Serving Learners at a Distance:
A Guide to Program Practices

by Charles E. Feasley

ASHE-ERIC Higher Education Research Report No. 5, 1983

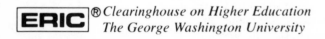
Prepared by

® *Clearinghouse on Higher Education*
The George Washington University

Published by

Association for the Study of Higher Education

Jonathan D. Fife,
Series Editor

Cite as:
Feasley, Charles E. *Serving Learners at a Distance: A Guide to Program Practices*. ASHE-ERIC Higher Education Research Report No. 5. Washington, D.C.: Association for the Study of Higher Education, 1983.

The ERIC Clearinghouse on Higher Education invites individuals to submit proposals for writing monographs for the Higher Education Research Report series. Proposals must include:
1. A detailed manuscript proposal of not more than five pages.
2. A 75-word summary to be used by several review committees for the initial screening and rating of each proposal.
3. A vita.
4. A writing sample.

ISSN 0737-1292
ISBN 0-913317-04-7

ERIC' **Clearinghouse on Higher Education**
The George Washington University
One Dupont Circle, Suite 630
Washington, D.C. 20036

Association for the Study of Higher Education
One Dupont Circle, Suite 630
Washington, D.C. 20036

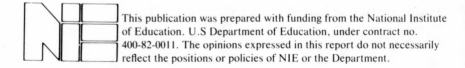

This publication was prepared with funding from the National Institute of Education. U.S Department of Education, under contract no. 400-82-0011. The opinions expressed in this report do not necessarily reflect the positions or policies of NIE or the Department.

CONTENTS

FOREWORD

Traditional higher education institutions have historically offered formal training beyond the bounds of their campuses. Early on agricultural extension agents were used by land-grant colleges to reach U.S. farmers. However, in the 1960s when campus enrollment was high, it was not American but European universities, especially in Great Britain, that set new standards and improved techniques for distance education.

Distance education has higher institutional priority in the 1980s. There are several reasons for this. First, as traditional campus-based enrollments of 18 to 22-year old students decline, institutions need to "broaden the net" to survive. This is especially true for institutions located in rural areas where the general local population, regardless of age, is not sufficient to maintain educational programs. Second, more older students desire to continue their education, but employment and/or family obligations limit their willingness to take on the time and residency requirements of full-time on-campus students. To reach these older students, institutions may be forced to develop strategically placed distance education programs. Third, institutions need to increase productivity. It is felt by many that the use of new technologies—especially television, video tapes, and video discs—will require fewer resources to reach a greater number of students.

While today there is a higher priority for distance education and a greater acceptance of its academic credibility, there is limited knowledge concerning the differences between successful campus-based programs and successful external offerings. A considerable number of publications have addressed these issues but much of the literature is unknown to American higher education since it was conducted outside the United States. It is for this reason that Charles E. Feasley, Director, Independent and Correspondence Study Department at Oklahoma State University, has prepared this Research Report.

Dr. Feasley has reviewed more than 140 publications concerning distance education and has developed an analysis covering basic five areas: student participation, faculty issues, the technology of delivery, necessary support systems, and the organization and process of distance education. This report will serve well as a primer for those institutions and academic programs that are beginning to look at distance education as an important priority.

Jonathan D. Fife
Director and Series Editor
ERIC Clearinghouse on Higher Education
The George Washington University

ACKNOWLEDGMENTS

I am grateful to my late father for his continual support and teaching of the importance of detail; to Barbara Adams for her very capable assistance in preparing the manuscript; to Barbara Fishel for her editing of the manuscript; and to Sue Feasley, Hyman Field, Jonathan Fife, Jill Holmes, Ray Lewis, and Frank Nelson for their valuable comments about it.

EXECUTIVE SUMMARY

The Carnegie Commission on Higher Education predicted that by the year 2000 over 80 percent of off-campus instruction and 10 to 20 percent of on-campus instruction will use information technology (1972, p. 1). During the next decade, as the size of the traditional college-age population drops and the use of technology rises, it will be possible to provide education to many distance learners (individuals who interact with faculty physically removed from them using preproduced course materials). Because only 4 percent of U.S. workers' tuition benefits are now used (Smith 1980), the possibility of stimulating increased enrollments in distance education is enormous. As a result, many of faculty members' roles will be changed from dispensing information to codeveloping and/or monitoring distance learning resources. To properly reflect the extent to which research on distance education is evolving worldwide, this report summarizes an international array of literature.

Individuals who must learn at a distance have ongoing obligations . . . physical handicaps, or . . . live in geographically isolated areas

Why Will People Learn at a Distance?
Individuals who must learn at a distance have ongoing obligations (employment or caring for young children, for example) or physical handicaps, or they live in geographically isolated areas that prevent regular classroom attendance. Previous unsuccessful experiences in classroom settings compel some individuals to learn independently.

What Is the Role of Distance Faculty?
Distance faculty members are commonly called mentors or tutors, because they direct students to learning materials and personnel, provide emotional support, and evaluate students' progress. Although most individuals who "teach" at a distance spend a majority of their time with classroom courses or noneducational responsibilities, these multiple assignments have distinct advantages. Most importantly, the approval and continued credibility of distance education stems from the participation of regular faculty. Furthermore, the employment of practicing professionals as distance teachers increases the relevance of instructional materials.

Which Media Do Distance Learners Use?
Trends in distance education include (1) an increasing tendency for the same institution to use multiple media to

meet the needs of diverse students; (2) a decreasing reliance on broadcast media in favor of recorded materials; (3) a greater reliance on less expensive, less complex media; and (4) a wider assortment of options from which to choose (broadcast television and radio, limited circuit television and radio, audio- and videocassettes, videotex, computers, correspondence, videodiscs, telephones, for example).

How Important Are Support Services for Students?
The more that distance learning expands students' heterogeneity, the greater the need for nontraditional recruitment, admissions, registration, and counseling. Some of the more successful services include opportunities for students to build confidence, refine goals, and help one another. Researchers do *not* agree on the need for at least one class meeting per course or the establishment of regional study centers.

Can All Curricula Be Learned at a Distance?
Some courses, such as those that require laboratory work and psychomotor skills, present logistical difficulties to learning at a distance. The lists of subjects unsuitable to distance education is shrinking almost year by year, however (Neil 1981).

How Should Distance Education Be Organized?
Units that provide distance instruction are either autonomous institutions or wings of traditional colleges and universities. The main conclusions of a major study of nine diverse, autonomous distance universities are that such institutions (1) are more advantageous to students' external needs, (2) exhibit more efficient administration for the number of enrollments generally needed (9,000 to 22,000 a year), and (3) are less likely to compete needlessly with other distance units (Keegan and Rumble 1982, p. 245). Not everyone agrees, however.

How Important Are Planning, Management, and Evaluation?
Because students and faculty are physically separated, course materials must be carefully planned to accommodate complex delivery systems and methods of evaluation.

The development and delivery of courses are iterative processes constantly improved by diverse academic and nonacademic specialists working together.

How Should Distance Units Be Funded?

The high fixed costs of distance education departments call into question the use of standard criteria for funding—full-time equivalent enrollment, staff-student ratios, and contact hours. Careful planning can achieve the desired economies of scale and avoid duplicated efforts. Incentives are necessary so that institutions will select the least expensive, least complicated delivery systems.

What Are the Implications?

As technology increasingly affects postsecondary instruction, faculty members will acquire new skills to assume new roles in tutoring distance learners and developing materials that many institutions can use. Simultaneously, administrators will recruit many off-campus students by promoting the availability of diverse funding sources. Careful planning and evaluation of distance instruction will determine cost-effective strategies for delivery.

The strategy chosen for implementation of future distance education will affect students—and distance education itself—in certain ways:

- *Equity:* When students rather than the institution are expected to pay for home access to instruction (e.g., that delivered over microcomputer, videodisc, or cable television), the accomplishments of many years in providing equal educational opportunity may be undone.
- A *reduction in interaction:* If machines replace people without compensatory shifts in the remaining human teaching, the affective skills learned through modeling others' behavior will be partially lost.
- *The coordination of knowledge:* Without planning, knowledge will continue to be generated and distributed without regard to the types of ideas and skills needed or how they can be stimulated (Dede 1981).

WHO LEARNS AT A DISTANCE?

Distance education features noncontiguous communication between students and faculty within and about prepro-duced course materials (Holmberg 1980). In this report, distance education is identified by the terms distance learning, distance teaching, open learning, or extended degree program, which all signify greater opportunities for learning through innovative alternatives to regular class meetings.

Why Learn at a Distance?

All societies have problems that they believe can be resolved or ameliorated by education or training: (1) short-ages of instructional materials and personnel; (2) the inability to cope with a rapidly expanding population; (3) the inadequate provision for education of certain groups, such as the physically handicapped, prisoners, ethnic and racial minorities, housewives, senior citizens, and rural residents; (4) generally inadequate social services; (5) short-ages of certain skilled manpower; (6) the demand for retraining because of new technologies or other changes; and (7) an increased need for citizens' participation in community life (Neil 1981, pp. 64–68). A distance-learning system thus becomes an attractive complement to tradi-tional educational systems when many people cannot (or ·will not) use conventional systems to attack these prob-lems, especially if increased cost-effectiveness is expected.

The belief is widespread that the development, imple-mentation, and evaluation of distance-learning programs should be more responsive to students' needs and wants than those of traditional institutions. More than other adult students, correspondence enrollees seek certifying exami-nations and degrees (Glatter and Wedell 1971; Mathieson 1971). Students' reasons for learning at a distance include the ability to work at one's own pace, an enjoyment of learning alone rather than with others, and access to help in planning from institutional staff, which is not a feature of informal self-study (Flinck 1979).

Attributes of Distance Learners

Individuals in college-level distance education courses are substantially older than their campus peers (with a mean average age of between 30 and 35 years), and a majority have taken some previous college courses (Brown and Wall 1978). In general, the more prior education people have, the more likely they are to seek additional opportunities for learning, regardless of the way those opportunities are delivered. Of considerable importance to a campus-based institution that has its own distance learning unit is the frequency with which students are attracted to that institution by being able to learn entirely at a distance. Individuals who have been out of school a long time have fears about how well they will be able to perform in a classroom of "college-age" students. They want to build their confidence by mastering content in a personal, nonpublic setting. For example, students of the Extended Learning Institute of Northern Virginia Community College were twice as likely to be new to the institution if they were taking only distance courses (Bibb and Feasley 1981).

Many distance learning systems are designed to serve previously underrepresented groups of students. Although in some countries (such as Norway and Sweden), distance education is a universally recognized study form with students from all social strata (Holmberg 1980, p. 108), in other places progress in expanding access has been incremental. To illustrate, in the first year of the British Open University, only 10 percent of the students came from lower-class homes, while 10 years later over 30 percent did (Information Services 1981).

A 1977 survey of 11 institutions or consortia offering television courses observed that the representation of minority groups among enrollees was moderately lower than that of the surrounding population (Brown and Wall 1978). A larger study of 244 external degree programs throughout the United States, however, showed the student population to be 20 percent nonwhite, considerably higher than the national average (Sosdian 1978).

In a survey of 42 American and 15 Canadian correspondence programs, slightly more women than men were enrolled (Hegel 1981). In contrast, in distance education courses in Europe, a larger percentage of men were enrolled (Schramm 1977). The overall opportunities that women have within a society appear to be reflected in enrollment levels for distance education.

Potential Students
The greatest concentration of citizens who have experienced obstacles to further education is among females aged

25 to 34 who are married homemakers with children and males aged 25 to 29, usually fully employed with families. These potential learners are generally white-collar clerical or sales workers or unskilled laborers who usually have inflexible hours of work (Waniewicz 1979). Potential learners are trying to satisfy any of five distinct needs: (1) help in understanding the changes in one's own body and behavior produced by maturation and aging, (2) help in understanding the rapid technological and cultural changes of contemporary society, (3) skills for coping with the personal consequences of technological and sociocultural change, (4) new vocational skills required for a career change or pursuit of other new goals, and (5) guidance in finding meaningful and satisfying retirement roles (Schaie and Parr 1981).

Attrition
Completion rates can be measured by two major formulas. One approach calculates completions as a percent of all students who enroll for a course; the other approach deducts the number of students who do not complete at least one assignment (no-starts) from the total enrollees before calculating the percentage of completions (Mathieson 1971). In a comparison of the ranges of data from these two formulas, nonstarting students comprised 17 to 24 percent of distance students (Coldeway and Spencer 1980).

The use of the same formula to calculate completion rates at different institutions does not necessarily produce precise comparisons, because the formulas do not adjust for the percentage of applicants who are rejected. For example, while the completion rates for British Open University courses are about 70 percent, 50 percent of those applying to enter that institution are refused (Shale 1982, p. 117). In contrast, in a survey of 42 American and 15 Canadian correspondence programs, 70 percent had open admission with *no* requirement for a prior levels of education (Hegel 1981).

While much of the existing research indicates that students complete distance education courses less often (10 to 70 percent) than their counterparts finish classroom-based ones (50 to 85 percent) (Giltrow and Duby 1978; Hammer and Smith 1979), the percentage of completions for distance education can be improved. Many administrators believe that students are more likely to complete courses if they study at a steady rate and that a regular pace of study is more likely to be attained if the institution itself sets the pace. Furthermore, the more complicated the institution's support systems and use of media, the greater the need for group pacing (Neil 1981, p. 118). In a comparative study of completion rates in identical courses given on a self-paced basis versus on a semester schedule of dates, a regular rate of study was shown to have a positive effect on completing the course (Coldeway 1982, p. 33). Several researchers have observed that correspondence retention rates of 25 percent have been increased to about 65 percent with the addition of television instruction to the same course (Chamberlin and Icenogle 1975; Lipson 1977). In this case, the television lessons served as a mechanism for pacing (Brown 1975).

One of the more comprehensive reports of a distance program's ongoing study of student attrition (and what to do about it), which examined the status of 1,417 students 2.5 years after enrollment, found that:

- Almost 12 percent of the students did not submit a single assignment.
- The seasons of the year appeared to influence completions considerably, with the spring months and December being more difficult times to get started.
- Students' ages and levels of previous education correlated positively with successful course completion.
- The longer the delay after previous schooling, the less likely students were to complete courses.
- Reasons for students' withdrawal centered on various personal circumstances not under the control of the institution (although subsequent interviews elicited more criticism of the course materials, the tutors' work, and turnaround time for assignments) (Rekkedal 1982).

The results of two later experimental studies at the same institution are statistically significant. In the first study, students who had not submitted an assignment in the previous month were sent an encouraging post card, then letters, at one-month intervals. The response rate for this experimental group was 46 percent versus 31 percent for the control group. In the second study, the turnaround time for assignments (the time it takes for an assignment to go from the student to the grader and come back to the student) was reduced from a median of 8.3 days in the control group to 5.6 days in the experimental group by the use of on-site tutor grading, resulting in an increase in completion rates from 69 to 91 percent (Rekkedal 1982, p. 121).

In Canada, a comprehensive study of the relationship between 556 learners' personal attributes and their rates of completion showed that women were twice as likely as men to complete the courses (35 percent versus 16 percent) (Coldeway, Spencer, and Stringer 1980). Similarly, those who had previously completed distance courses or traditional postsecondary courses were more likely to complete successive courses. Age, time available for study, career goals, degree goals, and concurrent course enrollments did not affect students' completing courses.

In summary, present long-distance students do differ from on-campus students but not nearly as much as will potential distance learners. The important work remaining is to identify those students who will not be successful in distance education and to persuade them to choose the classroom instead.

THE FACULTY THAT SERVE DISTANCE LEARNERS

Attributes of the Distance Faculty

A survey of 569 faculty (tutors) from seven representative correspondence institutions in England shows the extent to which distance learning faculty may differ from their traditional counterparts (Harris 1975). Three-fourths of the tutors were men, one-tenth were retired from full-time jobs elsewhere, 99 percent of the faculty worked part-time, and 55 percent handled only one course. Fifteen percent of the tutors were under 30, and 28 percent did not have previous teaching experience (although they did have considerable professional experience). One-quarter of the faculty had written contact with 40 to 200 students in the previous two weeks, while, during the same time period, one-third of the faculty had written to fewer than five students.

A similar profile of distance learning faculty in the United States showed the overwhelming majority of instructors in noncampus colleges working part-time for those institutions. They came from three principal sources: other educational institutions, recent university graduates, and nonteaching professionals (Lombardi 1977, p. 48). Another survey of 57 correspondence universities in the United States and Canada found that in two-thirds of the institutions, under 50 percent of those who work with students in courses hold nonteaching jobs elsewhere (Hegel 1981, p. 30). When the distance education program is affiliated with a campus-based college, the institution's full-time faculty members are used in a preponderance of cases to teach (deliver) distance courses. The employment of regular faculty provides increased capability to secure approval for such courses from official faculty committees, to satisfy outside accrediting standards, and to match instruction to the college's overall objectives.

Yet using classroom-based, full-time faculty has some disadvantages. Frequently, the workload becomes excessive when the distance education course is added, diminishing the amount of time available for full-time classroom work and for professional development. The participation in distance education is not always adequately considered in decisions regarding promotion. The type of broad skills required of many distance tutors may prevent them from keeping current in specialty fields, reducing their attractiveness to other institutions for more traditional positions.

A . . . profile of distance learning faculty . . . showed the overwhelming majority . . . [to be] working part-time

Faculty Rewards

Individual faculty cite five major reasons for participating in distance education: (1) the desire to help previously unserved students; (2) the opportunity to work with certain kinds of students, especially those who may be practicing professionals in their fields; (3) the need to initiate or participate in a new program; (4) the prestige of assuming a challenging task; and (5) extra compensation (Medsker et al. 1975, pp. 178–79). However demanding overload assignments may be, many faculty find overload payments attractive even though pay for a distance education program is quite often lower than pay for the regular course load.

Faculty Roles in Delivering Courses

The faculty member responsible for delivering distance learning courses serves as a mentor who assists students in their independent learning. Such assistance might include answering students' questions as they use the standard instructional materials, directing students to appropriate additional resources, giving emotional support to students who want to continue or leave a particular course, orchestrating group and individual meetings with students when needed, and evaluating students' achievements.

Interaction between faculty and students occurs most often by telephone or mail. Each student's progress must be watched regularly. The faculty member must contact students who are not submitting work consistently, a practice that may be hard to do. At Athabasca University, for example, tutors contacted individual students fewer than once every two weeks (fewer than once every three months in the summer) and usually at the student's initiative (Coldeway, MacRury, and Spencer 1980).

Improving the quality of interaction between students and faculty is a common theme in the literature about distance education. One recent article, for example, details how to be a friendly tutor without altering academic standards, citing several examples of how to write a friendly introduction letter that encourages students to comment on their feelings about specific assignments and about studying at a distance (Lewis 1982). Other programs go farther than a cheerful letter of introduction. Coast Community College adds a photograph and biography of the faculty member. Institutions with substantial computer support systems, such as Miami-Dade Community College's RSVP, have been known to send birthday greeting letters.

Faculty have a role in relating a fixed course to different learners' evolving needs. At Northern Virginia Community College, audiocassette tapes are used to communicate personalized and extensive comments from faculty to students in courses like English composition. Faculty members' responsibilities in facilitating those evolving needs include keeping records, conducting face-to-face tutorial sessions, counseling students, using the telephone, and advising students about how to study (Lewis 1981).

Faculty consider providing feedback and motivating students as top priorities, but students in vocational and secondary school courses ranked tutors' corrections and comments as lower in instructional and motivational values than the text, self-check exercises, and assignments submitted for grading (Bååth 1980, p. 30). Tutors' efforts were also not very influential on students in a study at Athabasca University. Although an incremental pay scheme motivated tutors to provide a greater amount and higher quality of feedback to students, no significant differences were noted in completion rates or learners' performance (Coldeway 1980).

Although correspondence education writers for the past 90 years have stressed the need for motivation from distance tutors, in four areas the observed activities of distance learning staff do not reflect that belief (Bååth and Wångdahl 1976). First, even though frequent interaction between student and tutor is said to be desirable, a majority of correspondence institutions reported in a 1976 survey the use of more comprehensive instructional units than was the case 20 years ago. Within a course of fixed duration, the use of more comprehensive units reduces the frequency with which tutor and student interact. To compensate for the'resulting less frequent submission of assignments, marking by the tutor, and return to the student, regular telephone contacts between tutor and student should be maintained.

Second, the length of time from receipt of a student's assignment until its return with the tutor's comments varies widely, from 2 to 14 days. Third, despite the importance of well-trained tutors, few training materials exist;

even good job descriptions are lacking. Fourth, different people are used to grade assignments and to conduct face-to-face sessions. Using the same person in both roles would improve interaction between students and the institution.

Faculty Roles in Developing Courses

The role of faculty or the division of labor in the development of a course varies greatly among institutions (Field 1979, p. 66). The involvement of faculty in course development at a particular college or university is the result of a combination of conditions: the extent to which existing materials can be used, the expectation that other faculty and/or instructional specialists from the same or other institutions must be involved, the media that are used to deliver the instruction, and the relevant skills that the faculty member brings to the process (Lewis 1983, p. 48).

A faculty member should be involved from the beginning of course development to help select the media that will be used. The faculty member can adapt materials from elsewhere or originate material because he or she is competent in the subject area and has considerable experience in teaching. Faculty thus involved in development are more enthusiastic about the course, and that positive attitude is transferred to students.

Because distance learning courses are designed with few or no class meetings, the packet of materials for these courses (sent immediately after enrollment) must be as self-explanatory as possible. They must tell the student about *everything:*

- what books to buy and where to buy them;
- what the course assignments are, when they must be submitted, and the criteria for their evaluation;
- what process to follow to withdraw from the course and to qualify for any refund;
- what kinds of questions will be in course exams, when to take the exams, and where to take them;
- what opportunities are available to contact the faculty member for questions about course content;
- which individual(s) should be called about administrative problems or inquiries; and
- what the grading scale is within the course (Field 1979).

In addition to using formats for the materials that compel the student to respond actively to the concepts presented, the writer of the materials must anticipate commonly asked questions. Past teaching experience in the classroom helps a faculty member identify and address such needs. As much as the pacing of the instruction permits, discussion pertaining to these common questions must be included.

Because materials for distance learning are much more accessible to review by other faculty members and the general public, they are scrutinized even more stringently than materials used in the classroom (Hewitt 1982, p. 63). It often happens that the standards required of students as stipulated within the materials for distance learning are intended to impress colleagues more than serve students, perhaps because a faculty committee or department head must approve the material. Material is frequently adapted from courses at other institutions, and six factors can help a faculty member decide whether or not to adapt a given course: (1) fit with the curriculum, (2) appropriate content and level, (3) length, (4) diversity and completeness of media, (5) availability and lifetime, and (6) quality (Daniel and Forsythe 1979).

Training and Scheduling Faculty
A number of strategies can make faculty members' involvement in distance learning more effective:

- making provisions for active oversight by departmental faculty;
- encouraging the participation of prominent faculty members;
- using full-time rather than part-time faculty as much as possible;
- using technology in the least complicated and obtrusive way;
- targeting the use of technology to save time for faculty members; and
- offering an effective orientation program (Lewis 1983, pp. 50–51).

An examination of 16 extended degree programs reveals a variety of strategies for faculty development and evaluation: rotating committee assignments; creating internships;

scheduling orientation meetings and manuals; encouraging new faculty to work with experienced faculty; initiating faculty exchanges with other institutions; sharing ideas through workshops and retreats; and evaluating performance through interviews, surveys, and analysis of documents (Medsker et al. 1975, p. 189).

Unfortunately, few detailed descriptions exist of training programs for faculty who work with students at a distance. One case study describes three different approaches that have been used at Athabasca University to develop and increase tutors' communications skills. The earliest approach was a two-day workshop, followed by analysis of a number of tape-recorded telephone calls between tutors and learners in which tutors tried to apply the model of problem solving they had learned in the workshop. In response to participants' evaluations, the second approach included one seven-hour training workshop, subsequent individual analysis of self-recorded telephone conversations with learners, and another group workshop of several hours to comment on the process and to practice the techniques they had learned. In general, the tutors became more active listeners, paid greater attention to what they said to learners, and made learners more responsible for their own learning. The third approach, which has not yet been fully evaluated, is to replace the initial workshop with a home-study course (Cochran and Meech 1982).

General purpose handbooks to assist faculty members in writing and using materials for distance learning commonly include topics such as the target audience, format, style, active learning, use of media, and readability. Using the instructional strategies of advance overviews, summaries, pretests, objectives, and inserted questions can help faculty members to select appropriate formats for learning materials (Marland and Store 1982). To train faculty in teaching courses, examples of tutors' comments that are especially motivating to students are helpful; they include the use of first names, the expression of confidence in the student's ability, comparisons to the instructor's past experiences, and a willingness to help the student in any way (Estabrooke 1981).

Careful planning is essential in determining and adjusting a faculty member's total workload during development or delivery of a course. Assigning regular faculty to distance courses requires negotiations with the directors of regular academic departments or divisions regarding the proportion of time to be devoted to distance education. The time the faculty member will require to complete each task must be estimated: reviewing existing materials, preparing new materials, grading assignments, and interacting with students. During the time students are enrolled in the course, the workload for the faculty member must be directly related to the number of students in the course at that time. Of course, the demands upon the faculty member's time will vary according to the extent to which his administrative responsibilities can be delegated to others. Assistants, for example, can help with grading during the course, and students can be given the name of another source to contact with questions.

THE MEDIA THAT DELIVER INSTRUCTION TO DISTANCE LEARNERS

In these times of considerable concern about providing cost-effective educational programs, the selection of media to deliver instruction must be based on what costs least, is least complicated, is most accessible, and still produces the desired results. Various ways to deliver distance instruction are possible, and each has its advantages and disadvantages.

Print

In many cases the best medium may be print. Besides being very familiar to almost all learners, it is inexpensive and portable. Because the format of print is a fixed presentation, students can look at any part of the message in any order for any length of time. Further, print materials are easily distributed to learners through existing mail and package delivery systems.

Print correspondence study has provided many students with opportunities for helpful interaction with faculty members. An estimated three million students are enrolled in correspondence education or training in the United States (Bååth 1980).

Broadcast Television

The use of broadcast television by postsecondary institutions is widespread and diverse although frequently supplemented by ways to interact with the faculty member. Of approximately 2,800 U.S. colleges and universities, 71 percent reported some use of television during 1978–79. Twenty-five percent of responding colleges and universities (735) reported offering 6,884 credit and noncredit courses over television to half a million students. Fifty-two percent used television for instruction given on campus, 14 percent for instruction given off campus, and 32 percent for noninstructional programs. Some researchers have found dramatic improvement in completion rates of correspondence courses with the addition of regular television broadcasts (Lipson 1977), and a weekly newspaper article or television lesson can serve to pace many students through the correspondence material.

A variety of cooperative arrangements are used to deliver off-campus instruction. Almost 60 percent of the institutions using television for instruction worked with public television stations, 24 percent worked with cable television systems, and 18 percent cooperated with commercial television broadcasters. In addition, almost 30 percent of the colleges and universities using television for instruction were members of consortia offering or producing courses (Dirr and Pedone 1980). The factors of greatest help to such consortia include (in descending order): quality of instructional materials (learner appeal, academic content, production quality, and instructional design); positive relationships between station and college; commitment of leaders; learner-centered focus; supportive context for distance learning (government policies at various levels that facilitate access, flexibility, and outreach); governance; stability (firm financial and legal basis for long-range planning); and system links (mechanisms for communications and lobbying) (Munshi 1980, p. 42).

As a particular example of such cooperation between stations and institutions, the Public Broadcasting System has recently begun to offer via satellite various television-based courses produced by colleges and universities on its network service aimed at adult learners. During the network's first year (1981–82), 555 U.S. colleges and universities (slightly more two-year than four-year institutions) cooperated with more than 80 percent of the public television stations in the country (in 47 states), offering those courses to over 50,000 students (Reed 1982).

In the future, many students will have easier access to expanded broadcast offerings through low-power television and direct-broadcast satellites (Norwood 1981). Low-power stations can be constructed for as little as $50,000, in part because the government does not require production facilities for local programs. Thus far, the Federal Communications Commission (FCC) has approved only a small number of such stations in rural areas. The local distribution of educational programs produced elsewhere would increase the opportunities within any television area. The FCC has also authorized eight companies to use satellites to broadcast directly to homes in the United States. National or regional groups of colleges and universities could contract with such companies for the distribution of programs to homes; such programs would be used within courses offered at those colleges and universities.

An early review of 421 comparisons of instructional television to live classroom instruction in a variety of

. . . the selection of media to deliver instruction must be based on . . . costs . . . accessib[ility], and . . . results.

subject areas found that students at all grade levels learn as well in both settings (Chu and Schramm 1967). Yet the greater cost of and planning time needed for television have stimulated efforts to identify those instructional tasks that are done much better or only by television. For instance, television is particularly well suited for magnifying images, providing slow-motion or repeated action, and combining the images of things that do not naturally appear together (O'Rourke 1980). Further, while motion or color within a program affect learning, they do so only if they are a critical part of the concept to be mastered (O'Rourke 1980).

The British Open University has used several means of increasing students' awareness of the functions of television broadcasts and the benefits received from them. First, tutors at regional learning centers are encouraged to organize special viewing sessions and discussion groups before the broadcast to emphasize the need to prepare for the programs. Second, faculty are instructed on how to prepare broadcast notes for students' use, including an explanation of the role that broadcast programs play within the course, the way that students can be made active learners during the broadcast by having them answer a question raised during the program or take a reading from an experiment on the screen, and the use of postclass activities like criticizing opinions expressed in the program or discussing the relationship between information in the broadcast program and that found in other course programs (Kern 1976). Third, the preparation of a video program and accompanying written materials can demonstrate and explain different ways that television is used for instruction: to follow a process or argument, to provide a specific experience such as a drama, to offer case studies, and to involve students in an exercise (Durbridge 1981).

Even within television programs designed to accomplish the same instructional function, careful research can aid in the preparation of materials that will have the greatest impact on students. Baggaley and Duck (1977) described the results of six experiments that examined the effects of particular television production techniques. The edited insertion of different audience reaction shots significantly affected the presenter's intelligibility, interest, and expertise. When viewers saw a presenter with prepared notes, that person appeared less fair and more confusing. When a presenter addressed the camera directly, the viewers considered that person significantly less reliable and expert than when seen in profile.

Videotape and Videocassette
Because television does not halt for students' questions or adjust to individual differences, videocassettes have become a substantial portion of the media used for distance education. Videocassettes are relatively inexpensive, easy to use, and generally compatible with many different manufacturers' players, and many companies have begun to use them for employee training and marketing (Norwood 1976). Professional associations' use of videocassettes is also extensive and growing. For example, 60,000 attorneys in California use cassettes on new legal developments that have been prepared by a self-supporting unit of the state bar association. The national American Bar Association's Consortium for Professional Education has more than 200 videotapes with programs ranging in length from 20 minutes to 12 hours (Hamblin 1982). Very recently, videolaw seminars, featuring two-way audio and video interaction, were held in a few selected cities using the Bell System's Picturephone Meeting Service.

For almost 10 years, Stanford University staff have been providing companies with master's degree programs in science and engineering using videotape recordings of campus lectures for use in the companies' own plants (Gibbons, Kincheloe, and Down 1977). (Sections conducted by videotape generally have three to eight students, while on-campus sections are much larger.) An on-site tutor is selected from the participating company's staff. In most cases, the tutors are practicing engineers with no prior experience in teaching, but they are chosen because of sensitivity to students, an ability to draw students into a worthwhile discussion of issues, and a personal interest in reviewing the content of the course.

The tutors have three chief functions: to start and stop the videotape machine as needed for group discussion, to answer questions the class cannot resolve, and to obtain answers and supplementary materials from the on-campus instructor. The on-campus staff and the videotape tutor discuss students' performance on assignments and exams over the phone.

Individuals enrolled in the videotape course must submit the same assignments as classroom students; the same person grades both sets of assignments. Both groups of students take the same examinations on campus. After three years, 82 videotape students and 65 different tutors had been involved. The 48 videotape students who met regular admission standards performed better than the students in the on-campus lecture or live television lecture with audio talkback capability. Even the videotape students who did not meet regular admissions standards did very acceptable work.

Instructional Television Fixed Service

Instructional television fixed service (ITFS) is a low-power, all-directional broadcast system with a direct reception area of about 20 miles, which can be expanded by signal repeaters and linked systems. Equipment for ITFS costs about $2,000 per location. Each ITFS licensee is permitted up to four channels that could be used separately to serve different audiences simultaneously. The system also has a two-way audio communication option (using FM frequencies) that permits students and faculty to talk to each other. ITFS can be used in distance education in three ways: (1) providing a closed-circuit network for an institution with multiple locations; (2) feeding programs to a cable company, then to homes; and (3) linking a college or university to business, industry, or medical institutions. In contrast to conventional television broadcasting that must meet a few needs of many audiences simultaneously, ITFS can be "narrow casting" in the truest sense (Graff 1980, p. 58).

Although ITFS has been used at all educational levels and in conjunction with many other media, its use is far short of its potential. Although ITFS could reach 40.2 percent of the college population, only 0.4 percent are served (Curtis 1979, p. 51).

Satellite

Communications satellites with fixed orbits about the earth have been used to deliver video and audio signals among many locations over a large geographic area. The simultaneous transmission over a large area thus makes this very expensive educational resource cost-effective. In most cases, a local educational authority receiving the transmission gives some official recognition (such as credit) for a student's successful use of those resources.

Satellite television systems are of three functional kinds. The first, a point-to-point system, has a relatively low-powered transmitter that broadcasts over a vast area. Because its signals are very weak when they reach the ground, it requires an antenna about 85 feet across and expensive ($3 million) amplification equipment. The second, a distributing system, uses more transmitting power and concentrates on a limited geographic area, permitting an antenna half as large and much less costly receiving equipment ($400,000). The third, a system for direct home broadcast, uses very great transmitting power to permit the use of an antenna only 10 feet across. Such direct home broadcasts will be possible in the United States in the near future.

Several organizations produce, acquire, and distribute educational programs via satellites. In addition to the adult learning service of the Public Broadcasting System, college credit courses are also distributed over satellite by the National University Consortium, the To Educate the People Consortium, and the Appalachian Community Service Network. The Appalachian Education Satellite Network illustrates the growth in the medium. The network was created in 1973 by the joint efforts of a regional planning commission and local public educators in eight states. In the first few years, about 1,200 teachers received graduate credit from 13 institutions. As costs of delivery for the satellite system were comparable to campus-based courses and cognitive and affective outcomes were equivalent, the network was expanded to serve over 3,000 students enrolled in credit courses at 70 local colleges and universities during the 1981–82 school year. Courses are provided 64 hours a week to 20 community meeting sites and 220 cable systems (Lewis 1983).

Another recent development in the use of satellites has been the formation and operation of the National University Teleconference Network (NUTN), which links 66 universities and the Smithsonian Institution to offer noncredit programs in 38 states (Desruisseaux 1982). Educational institutions that want to lease broadcast time on a satellite and gain access to equipment that can transmit to and receive from that satellite can secure the assistance of universities already doing so (such as those institutions that comprise NUTN), or they can contact the owners of the equipment directly.

Cable Television
About one-third of all households in the United States have cable television, wired to one of over 4,000 cable systems. In communities with high percentages of cable subscribers, cable television is used as the primary method of educational delivery (Lewis 1983). Because systems in major markets were required to have at least 20 channels, cable television offers a considerable outlet for educational programs. The programming potential of cable television will increase further with the use of fiber optics to provide more channels and a clearer picture, as successfully demonstrated in Japan and Canada (Ruggles 1982).

Three levels of interaction are currently found in cable systems (Miller 1982). On the lowest level, viewers telephone their queries and comments to the originating studio. On the intermediate level, multiple originating sites (usually in public buildings) have capabilities for two-way video and audio. On the highest level, subscribers can make push-button responses that are recorded on a computer at the cable system's control center. Thus, viewers can take course tests at home or ask faculty members selected questions if they wish. This level of interaction is being used on the QUBE cable systems of Cincinnati, Pittsburgh, Dallas, Houston, and Columbus, Ohio.

PENNARAMA is a seminal partnership between Pennsylvania State University (PSU) and a statewide network of individual cable systems. The cable systems established a nonprofit organization to build and maintain the microwave relay system that connects the cable systems with each other. PSU has a separate unit that provides eight hours of programs each day. Other colleges and universities as well as divisions of PSU itself have contracted for the distribution of their programs on the state cable network (Lewis 1983).

Administrators of the largest distance education institution in Canada, the University of Waterloo, are making plans to use the new Canadian interactive television/ videotext systems, Telidon and VISTA. It will then be possible to provide students with rapid feedback as well as simulations with color and graphics (Knapper and Wills 1980, p. 13).

Teletext and Videotex
"Teletext" and "videotex" are the generic names of two new information services that employ adapted television sets. Teletext is a one-way broadcast television service of fixed schedule, while videotex most often uses voice-grade telephone lines for two-way (interactive) selection of information available at any time. At present, the most widely known use of teletext is to warn viewers of severe weather or a program schedule change by displaying one continuous line of explanatory text near the bottom of the television screen. The entire television screen can also be used to, receive text from a teletext broadcast service. In fact, up to 10,000 different pages (full screens of information) can be transmitted every 10 seconds. In contrast to teletext, videotex is more expensive because of its ability to provide a wider range of services. By using a hand-held selector, the viewer can request a particular screen, with a maximum of 350,000 pages currently available on a system (Woolfe 1981).

Videotex can be used in a range of educational services:

- as a complement to educational television listings by offering specialized schedules organized by subject area or grade level, program notes, teachers' guides, or captioning for foreign languages;
- as an alternative to normal print processes by making available catalogs, bibliographies, or documents under development;
- as a disseminator of timely information by alerting users to job opportunities, community events, or consumer data;
- as the vehicle for interactive learning programs by allowing students to record their responses to course assignments and tests (Hurly, Hlynka, and Hurly 1982).

Despite this promise, the impetus to make videotex services available will have to come from the educational sector, because entrepreneurs will not invest additional resources for an educational market that is institutionally and politically fragmented (Hurly, Hlynka, and Hurly 1982). Because private industry is a large developer and user of training programs, it is possible that industry rather than traditional colleges and universities will first use videotex. Residential and business uses of videotex are being tested in France, Japan, Canada, and Britain; those trials will help determine the future educational market for the medium, and the residential trials in France and Japan are likely to lead more quickly to the development of distance learning opportunities (Ruggles 1982).

Videodisc
The need to provide a variety of learning paths for an increasingly diverse student population has led to the use of a microcomputer to provide alternate routes (branching) through a videotape program or the greater selections of a videodisc (Szilak 1979). A videodisc looks like a phonograph record; each 30-minute side contains 54,000 frames of pictures. A low-power laser beam scans the microtracks of the disc and changes the signals into a television picture that is fed into the antenna terminals of a television receiver. Videodiscs have greater storage capacity than videotape.

It is far cheaper to produce videodiscs in mass quantities than videotape (Graff 1980), yet to realize such cost savings requires easy access to disc mastering. At the beginning of 1983, only a few plants in the United States could produce a disc master, with a turnaround time of about four weeks. In contrast to videotape recorders, videodisc equipment cannot collect programs from a home television set. Until recently, videodisc could not be reused for another program, but the Japanese public television authority has now produced a videodisc on magnetic tape.

In contrast to consumer (capacitance) models, educational/industrial (laser) videodisc machines have greater learning advantages because they have the capabilities of freeze frame, slow motion, and search (Ruggles 1982). The interactive use of videodiscs has some major difficulties, however: costs of equipment, inadequate reliability of the hardware and software, complexity of the instructional program, and difficulty in revision (Hiscox 1982).

Computer

The two chief categories of computer use for distance learning are computer-assisted instruction (CAI) and computer-managed instruction (CMI). In CAI, students interact directly with a computer; in CMI, students do not communicate directly with the computer.

One of the more noteworthy systems of CAI is PLATO, developed at the University of Illinois. Its greatest assets include (1) remarkable graphing capabilities, (2) access to the calculating speed and power of a large computer, (3) heat-sensitive terminal display screens that can trigger random access audio and video in response to a finger touching the screen, and (4) terminals that can operate anywhere a telephone is available. In response to the high costs of long-distance telephone connections, regional networks of hardware and software have emerged, diminishing the cost. Because the highly versatile PLATO terminal is also quite expensive, PLATO software is being made available for use on microcomputers.

While CAI serves distance learners through direct interaction with the computer, CMI accomplishes a great deal without requiring computer access by the student. CMI has the ability to (1) present alternative goals that students select to determine their learning paths; (2) continuously monitor and assess how much practice a student requires, how well information is retained, and what methods of study work well; (3) use previous performance data to prescribe specific methods of study or testing; and (4) provide the instructor with group and individual statistics to help in the revision of course materials (Cooley and Glaser 1969).

Especially within distance education programs, communication between faculty and students that satisfies those functions of CMI can have considerable impact in motivating students to be capable, independent learners. Feedback on students' performance has the greatest impact if it is prompt, clear, and carefully written to be motivating. A CMI system known as CADE was introduced at the Hermods Correspondence School in Sweden in 1970 to provide such feedback specifically in response to some important observations. First, although students rated the assignments to be submitted as the most stimulating part of a correspondence course, they viewed the

The two chief categories of computer use for distance learning are computer-assisted instruction (CAI) and computer-managed instruction (CMI).

tutor's corrections and comments as the least stimulating part of the course. Second, a majority of students preferred receiving a simple answer key rather than instructors' corrections and comments (Bååth and Månsson 1977). The authors hypothesize that students expressed a very positive attitude toward the new CMI system because they preferred legible, computer-printed comments (in contrast to handwritten ones), the detailed comments that were given (300 words by the computer versus 20 to 50 by the live faculty member), and the fact that the computer never gets tired or angry (p. 38).

CMI is used in many ways in distance education. The educational broadcasting network, TV Ontario, has used a computer-managed learning system (RSVP), which operates on a fairly large and expensive computer, to write individualized letters to students who submit answers for multiple-choice questions. The letters clarify concepts, spur further questions, recommend related activities, and assist in gathering discussion groups by finding groups of students with similar problems (Waniewicz 1981). An important derivative of Miami-Dade's original development of RSVP has been the production of a similar microcomputer-based CMI system (Camelot), which operates on a small microcomputer and promises to make it financially possible for more institutions to serve individual distance learners. Finally, by placing microcomputers on mobile vans, North Island College in British Columbia has brought computers to even the smallest of its students' home towns.

An analysis of 54 studies comparing computer-based instruction (CBI) with conventional classes on examinations at the college level found some significant differences, the most important of which is that the computer produced about a 25 percent savings of time spent in instruction (Kulik, Kulik, and Cohen 1980). The computer's advantages thus lie in saving time and allowing more individualized instruction.

When distance learning institutions expect students to have their own computers, those students receive electronic mail or participate in computer conferencing. While electronic mail is a new mode of telecommunications for private messages between individuals, computer conferencing is a system for public communication between two, some, or all the members of a group (such as students in a college course). An extensive case study of over three years' experience by over 100 faculty members on a computer conferencing network at the University of Michigan explicated a wide variety of instructional uses. Included among the kinds of messages sent within the computer conference of a course were assignments for students, students' responses to discussion questions, and revisions of the syllabus. Because students' comments had to be typed for recording, students had to organize their thoughts much more carefully than they usually do in classroom discussions. Furthermore, shy students could carefully prepare their remarks at a comfortable rate. Where students' interest is likely to be the highest, such as at the graduate level, students can discuss the subject between class sessions. Student group projects, interdisciplinary team teaching, and academic advising by several individuals are also facilitated by computer conferencing. The chief obstacles to its use appear to be access to a terminal, the costs of implementing and operating the system, computer phobia, and faculty members' reluctance to try something new (Heydinger 1979).

An extensive examination of the time and financial costs of computer conferencing networks demonstrated that such communication among most groups of three or more people will become more cost effective than mail or long-distance telephone calls within this decade. Those factors examined include typing speed, terminal entry speed, speaking speed, computer processing time, printer time, computer cost, and personnel costs (Hiltz and Turoff 1978).

Telephone
The most frequently used technology noted in a recent survey of 70 exemplary programs for serving individual students off campus was the telephone (Lewis 1983). The major advantages of the telephone are low cost, ability to provide interactive instruction to isolated individuals, and flexibility. Students can talk to an individual faculty member or another student at fixed times or without prior scheduling. Telephone lines can also carry images of audiographic devices such as the electronic blackboard used for years by the Engineering Continuing Education office of the University of Illinois (Lewis 1983), the light

pen and scribble pad options of the CYCLOPS system at the British Open University (Sharples 1982), or the freeze-frame video used by the University of Wisconsin (Lewis 1983).

Consistent with its long-term commitment to statewide outreach programs, the University of Wisconsin has employed the telephone for instruction on a grand scale. The principal organizational structures used have been the Educational Telephone Network (ETN) and the Statewide Extension Education Network (SEEN). ETN has joined 210 meeting places in 100 cities and towns (Jackson, Parker, and Olgren 1979). Each location has a loudspeaker and four microphones to allow for group discussion. Instruction has been available for 55 hours each week in 34 credit courses involving 50 faculty and 600 students. On the average, classes last 90 minutes and involve 100 students at a time. Two important conditions of operation are dedicated four-wire telephone lines and the use of good written materials. The university's costs are much below those of shorter courses or workshops (14 cents per student for development and operation). Overall evaluations of these telephone courses have been quite positive, with 88 percent of the students indicating they would take another course taught that way.

Another case study of the two Wisconsin telephone networks noted that only five percent of the educational offerings were credit courses (Elton and Carey 1981). All together over 1,000 faculty members serve over 33,000 engineers, teachers, physicians, nurses, librarians, lawyers, business people, and others. Nonsalaried administrators are used at each receiving site. The paid management team for the two networks consists of 22 people. Over half the operating revenues come from student fees and about 30 percent from state appropriations, with the remainder coming from grants and annual fees paid by outside agencies for staff training.

Some statewide audio networks are supported and operated cooperatively by multiple institutions. For example, the six Kansas Regents universities have offered a wide range of programs over the Kansas Regents network for more than a decade (Kruh 1982). Over 3,000 students are enrolled in credit or continuing education courses each year at any of 64 locations, which include public schools, social rehabilitation service offices, public libraries, community colleges, and the six originating state universities. The importance of careful planning to the smooth execution of audio network programs can be seen by looking at one kind of program. Enrichment courses for college credit have been provided to high school students in many rural sections of the state. Although the format of each course varies according to the design of a faculty coordinator, each week usually begins with about an hour's presentation by an expert accessible by telephone anywhere within North America. Then students are given an opportunity to ask questions of that expert, with the faculty coordinator moderating. Background material is provided to students before each presentation, and students write a short paper afterward. Students have spoken with famous authors and musicians. Famous scientists have talked about, among other topics, life on other planets and new sources of energy. Numerous experts have examined national and international politics. In some cases, videocassettes provide an added visual component to the audio network. This increasing use of audio teleconferencing stems from the discovery that for many communication tasks, it is as effective and far more economical than video technologies (Dutton, Fulk, and Steinfield 1982, p. 322).

An early case study of the use of the telephone in Europe was conducted at the·University of Lund in Sweden, where the telephone was used to enhance motivational feedback in an educational psychology course (Flinck 1975). Of particular interest was the discovery that in 10 percent of the phone calls, over half the content was personal counseling. In subsequent studies at that institution, telephone tutoring had a positive impact on students' performance in the final French exam but not in economics, with no reason being found for the difference in impact (Flinck 1978). In neither group was there a uniform reduction in students' feelings of isolation from others nor any impact from telephone tutoring upon the amount of time spent studying.

In the United States, however, one study reported on the positive role that use of the telephone can play in students' retention and performance (Anandam and Fleckman 1978). In an introductory psychology course that included a textbook, a study guide, a weekly television

broadcast program, a weekly radio broadcast, and the opportunity for students to phone in questions and comments, telephone calls were made to the 25 students who did not submit the first of six optional sets of study questions, which stimulated computer-generated comments on individual student's responses. Because submission of the first set of optional study questions was a better predictor of a student's completing the course than his or her sex, age, or attitude toward self-control of situations, the telephone calls played a role in increasing course completions. Six more students completed the course as a result of the telephone conversations' revealing that students did not understand administrative procedures of the course (Anandam and Fleckman 1978, p. 221).

Audiocassette

As the competition for limited instructional broadcast time becomes stronger and the rising cost of the broadcasts harder to absorb, distance learning staff have explored more ways of using audiocassettes. Audiocassettes have several advantages: they are readily available, relatively inexpensive, and portable, and students can stop and replay them at will. In one monetary economics course, for example, audiocassettes were used to explain the relationships among course modules, including optional ones. Audiocassettes were also used to explain the purpose and details of the evaluation questionnaire presented at each stage. About 10 percent of the students also followed the suggestion to record additional comments on the blank reverse side of the cassette. The chief modification in the course as it was revised was to increase the material on the audiocassettes, an action that stemmed directly from earlier evaluations in which 48 percent of the students preferred more audiocassettes. Results of a subsequent evaluation showed a higher satisfaction with the role of the audiocassettes (Stanford and Imrie 1981).

In another study of four social science courses, even students who prefer to use written information rather than audio tapes felt that the tapes fulfill a valuable role (McDonald and Knights 1979). While in this study 23 percent of the social science students replayed the tapes, in another more detailed study of the humanities course Images of Man, 91 percent of the students, on average, listened to part of a tape again (Gough 1980a, p. 9). Additionally, 70 percent of the times that a tape was being played, the student was also doing another unrelated activity, such as homework. (Because of repeated playings of a tape, the students claimed that 75 percent of those tapes were also played with no distractions.)

Thus, it is not unreasonable to conclude that a large proportion of recorded audio material is too slow in delivery and inappropriately phrased for efficient listening. If students are given freedom to stop, then speed up or slow down selected segments of a tape, they can effectively use variable speed (compressed speech) audiocassette players. For example, in a basic nutrition and food science course at Syracuse University, students who used variable-speed audiocassette players on seven instructional tapes saved, on average, 32 percent in time and achieved an average grade that was 4.2 points higher on posttest scores (Short 1977).

The British Open University has used audiocassettes extensively as a result of the planning to deal with limitations on available radio and television broadcast time. In addition to surveying students to determine their access to an audiocassette player (69 percent), staff members completed a cost analysis that led to the conclusion that the use of audiocassettes was cost efficient (and conducive to individual pacing) until the enrollment in a given course was at least 500 students, at which point broadcast radio was justified (Kern and Mason 1977).

Radio
Radio is so much a part of our environment that it is the wallpaper of American life and consequently is not thought of as a medium for instruction (Forsythe 1979). Another reason for the underuse of radio for instruction in the United States is that the natural evolution of radio as a tool for the extension of higher education was disrupted by the establishment of National Public Radio (NPR), which was initially developed by the Corporation for Public Broadcasting in collaboration with National Education Radio (an organization composed of 150 to 200 of the larger stations owned by colleges, universities, and public school systems). Not surprisingly, the criteria for receiving federal support from NPR paralleled the characteristics of Na-

tional Education Radio members, including their preference for cultural over instructional programming (i.e., an NPR station *cannot* have instruction as its primary activity) (Forsythe 1979). Consequently, reduced instructional radio activity was noted in a recent study of public radio stations (NPR Education Services 1982). While 40 percent of the stations offered instructional programs in 1978, by 1982 only 29 percent did so. Programs are rarely publicized beyond the host institution, which severely limits the drawing power to distance learners.

Radio has some pedagogical value. It can pace students through the instructional material of a course, provide feedback to students so that they have a sense of belonging, and update or correct existing materials. Primary resource materials, such as performances, speeches, and discussions can be brought directly to listeners, influencing the public at large as well as students. Radio can modify students' attitudes by presenting material in a novel or dramatic way or from an unfamiliar viewpoint (MacKenzie, Postgate, and Scupham 1975, p. 60).

A variety of uses of radio were observed in a detailed analysis of 191 Open University (U.K.) radio programs that had been broadcast for course use: discussing students' problems (5 percent of the time), assigning tasks to students (8 percent), alerting students to other broadcasts (6 percent), and reinforcing material in the course text (81 percent). Despite the diversity of content included in the courses, the format was consistently uniform. Two-thirds of the programs were lectures or interviews, while only 5 percent provided a critical or alternative viewpoint. Furthermore, the majority of programs required little activity from students (Meed 1977).

A good instructional radio program can require 18 months for development (Danna 1981). At the College of DuPage in suburban Chicago, for example, a faculty member begins to design the course in conjunction with an instructional developer, a writer, and a producer/director after a proposal for a course is accepted. Existing materials are sought before time is committed to the development of new materials. The planning also includes a decision on whether or not to use lectures recorded in front of a class rather than in a studio, and that decision involves handling announcements at the beginning or end of the class period, instructing the faculty member, who wears a microphone, to repeat students' questions, and having visual materials numbered and distributed in advance to radio students (Forsythe 1979). Finally, the course must be promoted, including announcements over other radio stations, in local newspapers and the station program guide, and through direct-mail brochures.

In a study of various educational radio programs in European countries, regardless of the value of programs, the work required of students in courses, or the transmission times of broadcasts, students' listening rates dropped about one percent per week from a high of 60 percent to about 25 percent in the thirty-third week. Furthermore, while students liked programs that were straight lecture, the distance learning institutions' professional staffs rated documentary programs as more valuable. Thus, the study pointed out the need to teach students the role of different kinds of radio programs (Bates 1982a).

Subsidiary Communications Authority
U.S. radio stations, with the permission of the Federal Communications Commission, may broadcast programs for a general audience over FM channels while simultaneously using a subchannel to deliver a subsidiary communications authority (SCA) program to a limited audience. To receive the subchannel a radio with a special decoder is needed; it costs about $75 and is less portable than regular receivers. Because SCA signals must be transmitted at lower power, reception is possible only for a much smaller area. Because capital costs for station equipment range from $10,000 to $100,000, only about 50 noncommercial stations employ SCA (Carnegie Commission 1979, p. 367).

SCA was first used in the United States in 1961 by the University of Wisconsin to transmit postgraduate medical programs over the state's FM radio network. Albany Medical College has been very active for 20 years in serving the medical staff at 70 hospitals and nursing homes in six northeastern states, using the main channel for instruction and the subchannel for viewers' questions to the presenter. In contrast to this use for professional education, SCA has enabled Ohio University to offer special programs to bus-riding high school students and other institutions to provide special reading services for visually impaired learners.

Summary

Several recent trends have occurred in the use of media for distance instruction. First, multiple media are being used more frequently within the same course by adding an interactive component to a one-way medium. Thus, the use of broadcast media solely is declining and the use of more interactive media increasing. Second, contrary to what would be expected from the high priority given to reducing institutional costs, the increased use of interactive media can raise the expense of equipment for delivering instruction as well as reduce the likelihood that the same telecommunications program (software) can be shared by several institutions to spread the costs. Third, the range of media options is broadening but unfortunately including more complex options as it does so. Not only is increased cost a characteristic of complexity, but so is the need for training to use the equipment, thereby reducing the control that the average faculty member has over course content. For example, the development of a computer-driven video disc might require a computer programmer, a video technician, and an instructional designer in addition to the faculty member. Fourth, accessibility to distance delivery systems may be becoming more a reflection of students' wealth than institutional commitment, especially when instruction is delivered by media like cable television, satellite television, or microcomputers.

SUPPORT SERVICES FOR DISTANCE LEARNERS

Support services for students are as important to extended degree programs as the curriculum and the delivery systems used (King, Sewart, and Gough 1980, p. 15; Medsker et al. 1975, p. 111). More than campus-based students, some distance learners lack confidence in their abilities to cope with college, possess atrophied skills in reading, writing, and studying, and are wary of a degree program that is "different." Many adults are not sure they are doing the "right" thing by returning to an educational setting after a long absence. In comparison to individuals who are current students of one educational level planning to enter another level, distance learners have more difficulty getting preapplication information and advice. They want to find out how their current abilities and potential compare with the institution's entry requirements and the skills that students must possess to remain in the institution once admitted.

In content areas like science that have changed more quickly than other subjects, students may show a greater lack of fundamental skills and understanding than their previous coursework implies. Adult learners may find it particularly difficult to write documented, academic essays if their major writing experience in the past several years has been sending an occasional personal letter. Entering students with extensive work experience may be accorded some kind of "expert" status without the institution's fully determining the extent of their understanding. Even without such reinforcement, students may try to generalize too much from their work environments (Knights and McDonald 1982).

Learning the meaning of academic jargon can also be especially challenging for a distance learner who may not have much interaction with fellow students. And after agonizing over whether returning to school was the right decision, students want to make sure that others view their degree with the highest respect and not as a second-class consolation prize.

An analysis of state and local surveys of adult learning needs shows that from 20 to 50 percent of nonstudents indicated the lack of time resulting from responsibilities at job or home was the largest barrier to their attending college (Cross 1978, p. 14). When this fact is coupled with the importance also given to the lack of child care and

Support services for students are as important . . . as the curriculum and the delivery systems used

transportation as barriers to enrollment, recruitment counselors have strong evidence that potential students would view the flexibility of distance education programs as a solution to many of their problems.

The character of the student support system results from the often long and complex relationship between the student and the distance institution. Because students' requirements of a support system are diverse, the system usually consists of a large number of small but highly interdependent components. The system must be sufficiently flexible and robust to survive in a learning environment that may be at best unsympathetic to even the most reasonable administrative requirements (Friedman 1981, p. 123).

The greater heterogeneity of distance learners in comparison to campus students therefore heightens the importance of nontraditional recruitment, admissions, orientation, registration, and counseling.

Recruitment

Common sources of attracting potential students are existing students or staff, faculty or counselors at another institution, an employer or employment agency, a friend or family member, and written brochures. A study of 11 distance programs shows the diversity of institutions' methods for recruiting students to television courses (Brown and Wall 1978). All institutions reported using only one method in common—brochures announcing the first offering of a course. In descending order of use, newspaper ads, television and radio messages, posters, news releases, and direct mailings were other promotional methods used by some of the institutions. The most successful methods were brochures and newspaper ads. The timing of announcements about courses varied from one month to six months before registration, with the longer lead time more likely to include a catalog of courses. Some institutions, such as Miami-Dade Community College, aim their announcements at various target groups, while other places, like Coast Community College, blanket the service district. Common methods for evaluating the effectiveness of various promotional strategies were to ask students how they heard about a course and code information on application forms that identified promotional mode (Brown and Wall 1978).

Admissions and Orientation

By identifying the educational needs and information-gathering habits of target populations, then using appropriate means of recruitment, institutions can increase the probability of admission for those individuals most likely to benefit. An assessment of a student's application will determine if the applicant is within the institution's defined target population and satisfies any formal academic requirements for entry. A procedure of allocation determines whether space remains within the program of study, including geographic access to special facilities such as laboratories.

While only 25 percent of the external degree administrative units in a survey of U.S. institutions had no minimum educational prerequisite for a student to be admitted to a bachelor's degree program (Sosdian 1978, p. 26), more recent responses from 57 university-level correspondence programs in the United States and Canada revealed that 70 percent of those programs did not require previous education for admission to correspondence courses (Hegel 1981).

The establishment of a completely open admissions policy can have significant implications for the way in which an institution commits its resources to provide for potentially large attrition rates. Preapplication guidance must assist the applicant in the choice of his course of study at the same time it makes the student aware of the personal, domestic, and economic implications of what often is an extended study program. Although information guides can answer general questions, many institutions devote considerable resources to face-to-face or telephone counseling sessions that address individuals' specific uncertainties (Friedman 1981, p. 127). Local and regional support facilities for students of the British Open University, for example, absorb 30 percent of that institution's recurrent budget (Kaye and Rumble 1981, p. 28).

After acceptance, universities aid students' adjustment in different ways. Deakin University in Australia uses an orientation program that provides an acculturation period of several months before instruction begins so students can organize their private lives and prepare for the demands of study. The program materials alert students to likely difficulties and available resources and give advice on study techniques. Students are helped to review their reasons for enrollment to build their confidence (Gough and Coltman 1979).

Faculty members frequently send welcome letters to students to describe course components, such as orientation or review sessions, tests, grades, books, and other media resources. These letters may also include a picture and biography of the faculty member. Subsequent letters or postcards from the faculty member may remind students of upcoming assignment deadlines and special related events.

Registration

Two major practices of course registration differ considerably among distance education programs: whether students can register at any time and whether they can register to sample courses without academic penalty. Although many extended degree programs that allowed continuous registration decided to abandon that approach because of the cost in staff time and paperwork, many other institutions provide this option with or without computer support (Medsker et al. 1975). Of 57 distance learning institutions in the United States and Canada, 83 percent permit registration at any time, while 25 percent allow telephone registrations (Hegel 1981). Registration can frequently be completed entirely by mail, with books and all needed materials being sent to the student directly. When distance teaching units are part of a more comprehensive campus-based institution, it is often possible for students to enroll in distance courses during regular campus registration.

Counseling

Institutions and agencies considering external degree programs should recognize that distance students' information and counseling needs are likely to be different from those of traditional campus students (Medsker and Edelstein 1977, p. 22). Faculty should play a major role in the counseling program, even greater than the one they typically play in on-campus programs. Administrative staff and other students can help with counseling (p. 25).

The Regional Tutorial Services unit at the British Open University is considered the secret of the total institution's success (Keegan 1981). The system's primary goals are to provide a continuity of concern and to prevent dropouts.

Each foundation course has a local tutor-counselor for every 12 students. Interaction among tutors and students occurs through correspondence, on the telephone, and at regional study centers. Tutors' grading patterns are monitored by a computer analysis at a regional office. The 13 regional offices are each responsible for about 20 study centers, which are usually rented from local colleges for night and weekend use by faculty (tutors) and senior counselors.

Such a local regional center serves four functions: educational advisement, access to a particular institution, student support, and community liaison (Meakin 1982). The staff members at the centers are seen as generalists, with the criteria for their selection being administrative skills, self-direction, interpersonal skills, knowledge of the total education system, and experience as a mature student.

Among the more flexible ways of providing a regional center to a geographically dispersed population is the mobile learning center of North Island College in British Columbia. Built on the chassis of a motor home, each mobile unit includes two or more study carrels, a tutor's station, file cabinets, library materials, audio- and video-cassettes, a microcomputer, and laboratory space (Salter 1982). Another method of reaching geographically dispersed students is the use of graduates' professional offices as an advisory network of regional centers (Smith and Small 1982).

Although the study center might be a convenient meeting place for the student and tutor-counselor, it appears that the use of the telephone and informal meeting places such as private homes—even the local pub—are more frequently used for this purpose (King, Sewart, and Gough 1980, p. 22). In fact, after observing that tutor-counselors operate effectively in certain areas without a center (such as northern Scotland and the Western Isles), the authors concluded that study centers are not necessary (p. 19). The use of telephone, radio, television, audiocassettes, computers, and written materials can be just as effective in counseling long distance students (Wertheim 1981).

The Role of Telephone and Computer
The principal methods of providing counseling services to distance learners in Australia, the United Kingdom, and

the United States are mail, audiocassettes, telephone, and face-to-face meetings (Thorton and Mitchell 1978). Variations in the use of the telephone include students' calling any time, written requests for faculty to return calls at specific times, connecting groups of students with loudspeaker telephones, conference calls from up to eight students' homes at once, and dial access to recorded information tapes.

Paraprofessionals can be used effectively in telephone counseling. The most valuable types of counseling center on exploring one's strengths and weaknesses, goal setting, and making decisions about careers. The similarity of counselors' demographic characteristics to students' socioeconomic status increases their credibility (Arbeiter et al. 1978).

Miami-Dade Community College in Florida uses its computer-managed instruction system (RSVP) to generate letters to students who need improvement in performance and/or attendance at scheduled meetings. The computer can assemble sufficient data for the faculty and staff to determine the importance of students' characteristics (such as whether they are faculty- or self-advised or possess language, reading, and mathematics skills) in their successful learning.

A computer has been used at the Fernuniversität in West Germany to provide preenrollment advice. A booklet describing courses includes a series of questions. After students submit their multiple-choice answers to those questions, the computer prints a set of stored responses prepared by instructors (Fritsch 1982).

Prior Learning
Some institutions assess students' previous informal learning for course credits. Assessment has two basic functions: (1) It identifies and supports the credibility of the awarded credit, and (2) it has educational value in itself and becomes an important aid to the student in determining his future learning objectives (Medsker and Edelstein 1977, p. 28). Such services are costly, however, because they are time consuming (p. 29). The publications of the Council for the Advancement of Experiential Learning detail the various policies and procedures to follow in conducting this kind of assessment.

Face-to-Face Sessions

Face-to-face counseling can include campus counseling centers, regional centers, and itinerant counselors (Thorton and Mitchell 1978). Many distance learning institutions have orientation sessions, voluntary or required, at the start of each course. Students who attend such sessions have higher rates of retention and achievement than those who do not (Bowlay 1980). Another study found that students who attended optional seminars in two courses did better in percentage of completions, average grades, and time needed to finish the courses than those who did not attend. It was not possible to determine, however, whether seminars attracted high-performance learners or whether seminars contributed to high performance. Students indicated that if the seminars were designed to be directly related to course requirements, up to one-third of those invited might attend, but many students made it clear they would not attend seminars just for an opportunity to socialize with others (Peruniak 1980).

Campus sessions can serve to review important course concepts just before students are given an examination. While faculty members at Coastline Community College are encouraged to offer such review sessions, they are told to avoid unrealistically high expectations because on the average only 20 percent of the students attend (Jelen and Hirschfield 1978, p. 6). Frequently, faculty make audiotapes of the review sessions for students who cannot attend.

Regular sessions between tutors and groups of students (tutorials and seminars) are held about every three weeks in the Flexi-Study system in the United Kingdom. Using materials that have been developed by the National Extension College, almost 100 local colleges of nondegree education for adults provide counseling, practical work, and examinations in addition to face-to-face sessions. Early indications are that students drop out at a higher rate than in evening classes but pass exams at a higher rate (Freeman 1982, p. 165).

One method of combining distance study with face-to-face sessions is to use concentrated residential courses. This approach has worked well in a variety of institutions, with most such courses being taken during the summer (Holmberg 1982, p. 37).

Student self-help groups are used at the foundation and postfoundation levels of the British Open University. Only at the initial level is the tutor-counselor a regular participant in such voluntary groups (Sewart 1975).

As illustrated by the contradictory evidence mentioned in this section, the necessity of face-to-face sessions and student support services for distance learning remains an unresolved question needing further study.

ORGANIZATION AND PROCESS

Organizational Forms

Distance education courses are offered by institutions that were established to provide only that type of instruction or as an adjunct of an existing campus-based college or university. Within existing institutions, distance learning courses may be offered through continuing education or special organizational units. Staff members of extended degree programs that were developed to be self-supporting found that administering distance learning through the institution's continuing education division was efficient and effective (Medsker et al. 1975, p. 163). Furthermore, staff in several institutions found that creating a new academic unit reduces the interest of existing staff and the pressure on existing academic programs to be responsive to new clientele, curricular innovations, and delivery strategies (p. 164). As a consequence, the goal of maximizing the program's flexibility to experiment must be weighed against the necessity of the regular faculty's participation to heighten the program's credibility (p. 162).

Three methods of organizing a distance education unit are possible. First is the network approach, in which a fairly small institution (such as John Wood College in Illinois) coordinates and uses the resources of a number of other, frequently diverse, institutions. Thomas Edison College in New Jersey, for example, certifies work completed entirely at other institutions. A second approach uses *many* community centers in conjunction with multimedia components within courses. Rio Salado Community College in Arizona and Coastline Community College in California are examples. Coastline has about one center per square mile of its territory. The third approach is individualized learning, characterized by Empire State College in New York, which permits considerable flexibility in the timing, location, and frequency of meetings with tutors to chart and complete contracts for learning (Kaye and Rumble 1981).

Planning

Planning, management, and evaluation are critical activities for the integration of diverse staff contributions into a comprehensive distance learning system. Such activities require a good data base.

General planning processes that involve subunits in decision making include seeking proposals from the staff to assemble an annual plan, then seeking comments to revise the plan. The time frame of this planning is flexible; the British Open University invites annual comments, while the Universidad Estatala Distancia of Costa Rica uses a five-year planning period (Kaye and Rumble 1981, p. 218). The scope of such planning also varies widely. Among the most comprehensive studies of students' demands and attitudes ever conducted to plan a distance learning system were those executed between 1970 and 1979 for the establishment of the University of the Air in Japan, which included experimental programs and interviews with 5,000 citizens (Sakamoto 1982).

Management and Governance
Requirements for management of distance learning institutions are very different from those of conventional ones. Much of the teaching process in conventional institutions is not managed at all, as the individual faculty member has almost complete autonomy regarding what he or she does in the classroom (Kaye and Rumble 1981, p. 197). At distance teaching institutions, however, course design, production, distribution, and delivery necessitate the integration of many academic and nonacademic specialists. These specialists can be integrated in three ways: the use of an academic course team, the establishment of an administrative project working group, and the appointment of people with specific responsibilities for coordinating efforts of organizational units. To provide for the timely decision making that is needed in an institution requiring considerable centralized integration, a unicameral structure of governance is more likely to be used. Senior administrative officers are given considerable explicit powers, although they vary from institution to institution (Kaye and Rumble 1981).

Cooperation with Other Institutions
Several educational institutions have made cooperative arrangements to facilitate the transfer of students from one college to another or to share resources. For example, students can be concurrently enrolled in a two-year college, North Island, and a four-year university, Atha-

basca, in western Canada. Many legally recognized cooperative groups, consortia, operate in the United States to share the costs of televised instruction.

Many other areas for collaboration exist, however: the production and distribution of learning materials, the provision of student services, general administration, and consultancy (Kaye and Rumble 1981). Consortia are valuable in their providing a forum for diverse participation in decision making and an organization for mutual support (Dolce 1981). They serve as bridges between different types of colleges to reduce territoriality and competition. Cooperative arrangements have provided opportunities for developing and influencing governmental policy on tele-communications. Consortia provide a useful service to members by publishing newsletters, sponsoring workshops and forums, and obtaining grants (Zigerell 1982). The successful consortia have not been imposed from the outside but have been viewed by the member institutions as the only way in which certain goals can be met.

It is not an easy task to bring together diverse institutions (Beaty 1979). The decision to collaborate leads to consideration of several functional matters: the structure of the organization, the funding of the organization, and the type of agreement that will bind the group. Governance in a small consortium usually consists of a coordinating committee with a representative from·each member institution. Larger consortia often elect a five- to seven-member executive council. Ongoing committees can address needs such as research or courses offered. Decisions of the whole group must be binding because if individual colleges retain veto power over decisions of the consortium, the life expectancy of the organization will be brief (p. 41). During the formative years of a consortium, it may be possible for a consortium coordinator, selected from one of the member colleges, to volunteer the time needed to administer the activities of the group. The more successful consortia have hired full-time or part-time administrators, however.

Requirements for management of distance learning institutions are very different from those of conventional ones.

Financing Distance Learning Programs

Sources of financial support vary widely among distance learning units. Diversity is great even within the same type of institution; for example, local government support for two-year colleges may range from 0 to 50 percent. Even distance learning units that depend to a greater extent upon student fees for operating funds vary widely. Within the 72 institutions comprising the National University Continuing Education Association, course tuition fees range from $18 per semester hour to $73 per semester hour and from $20 per quarter hour to $42.75 per quarter hour (Markowitz 1983, pp. 13, 14). Although all but two institutions levied at least one additional special fee, institutions varied in what they considered justification for a special fee. For example, 85 percent of the institutions charge a fee to extend enrollment in a course, but only 10 percent charge a fee for nonresident students (p. 8).

The cost of television-centered courses falls into three major categories that apply to all distance education systems: (1) the development or acquisition of instructional materials, (2) the development of a basic delivery system and its organization, and (3) the delivery of the instructional services (McCabe 1979, p. 30). The first two categories are fixed costs that must be shared by many students, while the third can vary greatly according to students' needs.

Serious reservations have been expressed about the variable cost factors that are often the basis for most public funding decisions: ratio of staff to students, contact hours, and full-time equivalent enrollment. More attention should be given to the preponderance of fixed costs needed for distance learning institutions that may require additional funding. For example, the fixed-to-variable cost per student of 2,000:1 at the British Open University is much higher than the ratio at a typical campus university (8:1) (Wagner 1977). Although the British Open University has achieved a recurrent cost per equivalent undergraduate that is about a quarter of that at conventional universities because of its large number of enrollments, further reductions in cost do not appear possible without changes in the patterns of expenditure within courses (especially for the use of media).

Comparing costs and benefits of diverse distance education systems is fraught with difficulty. First, what may be an expense under one system is not necessarily in another. Second, costs for the same service differ in different countries. Third, actual expenditures and estimated costs can vary widely. Fourth, activities of on-campus and distance learning students frequently overlap. Fifth, benefits to nonenrolled individuals, some of whom may be convinced to enroll later, are seldom determined. A review of several cost studies of distance learning institutions in the United Kingdom and Europe, showing how much diversity and complexity exist in the effectiveness of the delivery systems, points out that economic effectiveness should not necessarily be the determining measure of such systems (Lefranc 1982, p. 24).

Although many cost-effective, multimedia distance learning programs exist, it is disappointing that many such programs concentrate on higher-cost video technologies, often to the exclusion of lower-cost audio and print technologies (Klees 1975). The disadvantages of this one-sided concentration are clear. Much simpler video productions could be done for one-twentieth the cost, an expensive, high-quality production may not be easy to revise, and instructional opportunities are lessened when fewer courses are developed (p. 128).

Cost may also have a negative effect on the revision of materials. Because students learn and teachers teach in different locations, the instruction must be more carefully designed and developed than that developed for the classroom. Quite often this planning necessitates the use of a team of specialists. Consequently, it takes more time and costs more to develop the materials used for distance education. The added cost and time mean that material is revised less frequently.

Evaluation
Evaluation and research have greater significance to distance learning than they do to traditional education for four reasons: (1) Innovative proposals require more documentation; (2) the considerable fixed costs of production and distribution for distance learning systems mean that they are not easily revised and must be used for several years; (3) authors do not come in close contact with students who use the materials, making it hard to know when revisions are needed; and (4) visibility to the public reinforces the need for careful planning and analysis (MacKenzie, Postgate, and Scupham 1975, p. 46).

In general the focus of evaluation in distance learning programs, as in classroom-based instruction, is on the student or on the instructional process itself. Progress can be measured during the process to identify the need for adjustments in the process (commonly called formative evaluation) or at the end of the instruction to gauge the level of accomplishment (commonly called summative evaluation). A number of evaluation criteria can be used to determine the success of an open learning program: access, which can indicate how many and what kinds of people are served; the relevance of the distance education services to the community's needs and expectations; the caliber of student outcomes and program offerings; the program's cost effectiveness; institutional impact, which includes influences upon the goals, policies, and practices of other institutions and society in general (Gooler 1979); the time it takes to produce a graduate; and the number of graduates as a proportion of the number of students admitted (Keegan and Rumble 1982).

The most comprehensive individual course evaluation ever undertaken of a British Open University course notes that a first type of necessary evaluation is critical comment by experts in content and course design that occurs before students take the course (Nathenson et al. 1981). Students' tryout of the course material provides other important evaluation data. The student trial can be developmental testing before full-scale use or careful monitoring of all students for one or two years, with needed revisions leading to the program's being used for up to eight years. Feedback comes from computer surveys of students' opinions, analyses of students' assessment scores, and in-depth interviews with students and faculty.

Some sound principles that will be of considerable value to individuals who are beginning to evaluate instructional programs have been offered: start out simply, use a variety of existing instruments when appropriate, employ informal indicators of the program's success widely, begin activities on a trial basis, separate evaluation of the program from evaluation of personnel, and encourage program staff's and participants' widespread involvement in the evaluation (Lehmann 1981).

Accreditation
Special efforts are necessary to evaluate distance learning programs comprehensively and accurately for regional and

state accreditation. For example, important areas and factors to be considered for the institutions that are members of the National University Continuing Education Association include philosophy, mission, administration, staff, faculty, instruction, services, research, and methods of evaluation (Burcaw 1982, p. 203). An excellent example of a successful, comprehensive self-study using these standards is the report for the 1979 accreditation of the University of Minnesota by the North Central Regional Association (Horgan, Nelson, and Young 1979).

Further refinements in the accreditation of distance learning programs are the focus of an 18-month study to assess long-distance learning using telecommunications that will be completed by early 1984 on behalf of the Council on Postsecondary Accreditation and the State Higher Education Executive Officers Association. Task forces on accreditation, state authorization, legal issues, and technology are assisting a steering committee composed of key people in regional and specialized accreditation.

Comparisons with Campus Institutions

Comparisons between traditional and nontraditional institutions have proven invaluable in demonstrating possible strengths and weaknesses of distance education. For example, a comparison of the effectiveness and costs between a noncampus institution (Whatcom Community College in Washington) and three campus-based colleges of similar size found that the noncampus institution seemed to perform as effectively in most operational areas, performed no better in determining and satisfying the needs of target groups, and spent 10 percent less per student and six percent less per course than the campus-based institutions (McIntyre and Wales 1976). Unfortunately, many published cost comparisons are based on estimated costs, and the results of such analyses are therefore suspect.

Students' Assessment and Feedback

Before the final examination in a course, students are usually given informal exercises to complete for self-assessment. The various ways in which answers are given to students for these self-assessments have their advantages and disadvantages. Answers at the back of the book seem to work well with questions requiring lengthy work (such as calculations) that diminishes the possibility of remembering the following answer. Having to turn to the back of the book frequently is irritating, however. Answers can be shown out of primary sequence in some randomly designated order or in groups of questions of the same number, regardless of chapter, but these methods are difficult to revise. Answers at the bottom of the same text page (upside down or right side up) are less irritating than answers at the back of the book but reveal more subsequent answers. The use of a scrambled location for an answer, used in branching programmed texts, is irritating as well as hard to revise. In medical courses, it is common to cover answers in one color with ink of another color that is removed with a transparent mask overlay, but this method is costly to produce (Stoane and Stoane 1982).

Presenting the latent image of an answer next to the appropriate question that remains invisible until treated with a developing pen may be quite appropriate for distance learning although copies may take longer to produce and be somewhat more costly. This method has the advantage of providing a permanent record of how many options a student chose before selecting the correct answer. Another variation is a method using liquid crystals that has been employed in Japan; while the materials are reusable, a record of students' responses is not provided (Stoane and Stoane 1982). A scratch-off cover (like that used in instant lottery tickets) is a possibility. Answers can be provided on audiotape, although the sequence of answers can be lost unless they are identified. Microcomputers can be used to provide feedback, but not all students can afford the hardware and would have to go to a learning center to use one.

In the preparation of specific feedback to students' responses, certain basic assumptions must be kept in mind. Good feedback is an integral part of course design, providing immediacy, regularity, explanatory rather than judgmental comments, conciseness, and clarity. Feedback is people oriented and as such must include efforts to reduce students' defensiveness. The feedback, for example, must emphasize equality rather than superiority (Gibb 1961). Feedback can take the form of written, oral, and self-assessments and include examples of good pieces of work, comments about drafts and outlines, and information about the distribution of scores (Store and Armstrong 1981).

The formal grading of submitted assignments throughout a course, called continuous assessment, yields results informative to both students and faculty (Connors 1981). Some institutions—Athabasca University, Northern Virginia Community College, and Oklahoma State University, for example—have careful procedures that permit proctoring by a local educational official. The more often testing is proctored, the more likely the institution's credibility is to improve; of course, this consideration must be balanced against the difficulties students have in securing proctors. The ideal grader is an individual who helped design the course and who has worked with students in the course. It may be necessary to have a mechanism for monitoring the patterns of grading, however, which can be done by computerized scoring. The combination of diverse performances into one final grade through some weighting of proctored and unproctored work is usually needed to enhance the institution's credibility.

Examinations

One testing approach that offers promise for use with adult distance learners is the open-book examination (Francis 1982, p. 16). In addition to reduced anxiety and reduced need for memorizing factual material reported by students, researchers also noted reduced cheating. The exams that provided the least benefit to learners used multiple-choice questions to assess factual information, while the exams that were of the greatest value required students to prepare an analysis or synthesis of information (Francis 1982).

A more comprehensive study compared closed-book tests with open-book tests and take-home tests with regard to students' behavior and attitudes (Weber, McBee, and Krebs 1982). Sixty students were randomly assigned to one of three groups that took all three types of tests in a different sequence during the same educational psychology course. Because each test had ten knowledge and ten application questions, researchers could determine a knowledge score, an application score, and a total score for each test. Based on a statistical procedure that shows the probability of similarity of item responses for pairs of students (Frary, Tideman, and Watts 1977), cheating was no greater problem for take-home or open-book tests than for the closed-book test. While scores on the application questions were not significantly different for the testing modes, differences on total test scores and attitudes (about effort expended, cheating, anxiety, learning, and difficulty) were more favorable to the take-home and open-book exams, respectively. Both high- and low-ability students spent more time on the take-home test, which could explain the higher achievement (although the simple correlations were weak).

Research

An increasing number of centers are publishing research on distance education in postsecondary education, and most of them are located outside the United States. Research activities at the Fernuniversität in West Germany, for example, focus on four main areas of research: target groups, advising and supportng students, teaching and learning, and systems-related matters (Weingartz 1981). In the first area, typical projects try to analyze students' motives for enrollment or how students cope mentally with success and failure. The second area studies orientation materials and processes using various media and examines methods to improve two-way communication between student and staff. The third area includes research on the use of computer-marked assignments in various subjects, the advantages and disadvantages of a conversational style in course materials, and the special challenges of an individualized type of study. The fourth area includes studies of which media are appropriate for courses and the creation and evaluation of distance learning institutions.

Summary

Distance education units are more often planned and managed by partnerships of academic and nonacademic specialists than are campus-based units. These considerable collaborations arise because producing course materials for distance learning institutions is more lengthy and costly than for their campus counterparts. The integration of contributions from such a diverse staff depends upon systematic, research-based evaluation. The more common processes of evaluation include the continuous assessment of students' accomplishments and ongoing program self-studies, which are valuable for management and accreditation by external agencies.

SUMMARY AND IMPLICATIONS

This global analysis of distance education has shown the size, range, and potential impact of the phenomenon. Despite a strong trend toward the use of multiple media, the major way of providing distance education remains printed materials. Distance education is successful for many (but not all) students at various educational levels; it is used in many content areas in economically diverse countries.

It is only when enrollment is high that the use of technology, especially broadcast media, in courses becomes cost effective in comparison to classroom-based students' achievements. In many cases, broadcast radio or audiocassettes can be substituted for broadcast television, which is about five times more expensive. Yet careful planning by administrators and faculty is necessary to realize these savings.

Distance education will become much more prevalent in the future because society will place a higher value on reducing students' time away from work and on needless use of gasoline for transportation.

BIBLIOGRAPHY

The ERIC Clearinghouse on Higher Education abstracts and indexes the current literature on higher education for the National Institute of Education's monthly bibliographic journal, *Resources in Education*. Most of these publications are available through the ERIC Document Reproduction Service (EDRS). Publications cited in this bibliography that are available from EDRS include the ordering number and price at the end of the citation. Readers who wish to order a publication should write to the ERIC Document Reproduction Service, P.O. Box 190, Arlington, Virginia 22210. When ordering, please specify the document number. Documents are available as noted in microfiche (MF) and paper copy (PC).

Anandam, K., and Fleckman, Bess. 1978. "Telephone Dialogue Intervention in Open Learning Instruction." *Journal of College Student Personnel* 18:219–27.

Arbeiter, Solomon; Aslanian, Carol B.; Schmerbeck, Frances A.; and Brickell, Henry M. 1978. *Telephone Counseling for Home-Based Adults*. Princeton, N.J.: College Entrance Examination Board. ED 162 089. 71 pp. MF–$1.17; PC not available EDRS.

Bååth, John A. 1980. *Postal Two-Way Communication in Correspondence Education*. Lund, Sweden: University of Lund.

Bååth, John A., and Månsson, Nils-Ove. 1977. *CADE: A System for Computer-Assisted Distance Education*. Malmo, Sweden: Hermods Skola.

Bååth, John A., and Wångdahl, A. 1976. "The Tutor As an Agent of Motivation in Correspondence Education." *Pedagogical Reports* no. 8. Lund, Sweden: Department of Education, University of Lund.

Baggaley, John P., and Duck, Stephen. 1977. "Guidelines in ETV Production: Six Experiments." In *Evaluating Educational Television and Radio*, by A. W. Bates and John Robinson. Milton Keynes, England: The Open University Press.

Bates, A. W. September 1982a. "The Impact of Educational Radio." *Media in Education and Development* 15(3): 144–49.

———. 1982b. "Trends in the Use of Audio-Visual Media in Distance Education Systems." In *Learning at a Distance: A World Perspective*, edited by John S. Daniel, Martha A. Stroud, and John R. Thompson. Edmonton, Alberta: Athabasca University.

Beaty, S. V. 1979. "Forming College Television Consortia." In *Using Mass Media for Learning*, edited by Roger Yarrington. Washington, D.C.: American Association for Higher Education. ED 165 856. 82 pp. MF–$1.17; PC not available EDRS.

Bibb, John J., and Feasley, Charles E. 1981. "Demographic Data

on Extended Learning Institute Students among Northern
Virginia Community College Students, 1977–1980." Mimeo-
graphed. Annandale, Va.: Extended Learning Institute,
Northern Virginia Community College.

Bowlay, D. J. 1980. "Orientation Programmes for External
Students: Do They Work?" *A.S.P.E.S.A. Newsletter* 6:2.

Brown, Lawrence A., Jr. August 1975. *Learner Responses to the
Use of Television in UMA Courses.* Executive Summary no. 8.
Lincoln, Neb. University of Mid-America. ED 159 969. 36 pp.
MF–$1.17; PC–$5.49.

Brown, Lawrence A., Jr., and Wall, Milan. 1978. *Report of the
University of Mid-America Office of Marketing and Informa-
tion Survey of Institutions Offering Television Courses.*
Technical Report no. 4. Lincoln, Neb.: University of Mid-
America.

Burcaw, Susan S. 1982. "Standards for Independent Study: The
American Experience in Higher Education." In *Learning at a
Distance: A World Perspective,* edited by John S. Daniel,
Martha A. Stroud, and John R. Thompson. Edmonton,
Alberta: Athabasca University.

Carnegie Commission on the Future of Public Broadcasting.
1979. *A Public Trust: The Report of the Carnegie Commission
on the Future of Public Broadcasting.* New York: Bantam
Books.

Carnegie Commission on Higher Education. 1972. *The Fourth
Revolution: Instructional Technology in Higher Education.*
New York: McGraw-Hill.

Chamberlin, Martin N., and Icenogle, Darrel. November 1975.
"Courses from Television: Potential for International Educa-
tion." Mimeographed. Paper prepared for the Wingspread
Conference on the Media and World Understanding, Racine,
Wisconsin.

Chu, G. C., and Schramm, W. 1967. *Learning from Television:
What the Research Says.* Stanford, Calif.: Institute for
Communications Research, Stanford University.

Cochran, Bente Roed, and Meech, Alan. 1982. "Training
Telephone Tutors." In *Learning at a Distance: A World
Perspective,* edited by John S. Daniel, Martha A. Stroud, and
John R. Thompson. Edmonton, Alberta: Athabasca University.

Coldeway, Daniel O. 1980. *An Examination of Tutor Management Strategies for Use in Distance Education.* Edmonton,
Alberta: Athabasca University.

———. 1982. "Recent Research in Distance Learning." In
Learning at a Distance: A World Perspective, edited by John
S. Daniel, Martha A. Stroud, and John R. Thompson. Edmon-
ton, Alberta: Athabasca University.

A. Stroud, and John R. Thompson. Edmonton, Alberta: Athabasca University.

Friedman, H. Zvi. 1981. "Systems for Student Administration." In *Distance Teaching for Higher and Adult Education,* edited by Anthony Kaye and Greville Rumble. London: Croom Helm.

Fritsch, Helmut. 1982. "Industrialized Counseling." In *Learning at a Distance: A World Perspective,* edited by John S. Daniel, Martha A. Stroud, and John R. Thompson. Edmonton, Alberta: Athabasca University.

Gallagher, Margaret. 1977. "Programme Evaluation Methods at the Open University." In *Evaluating Educational Television and Radio,* edited by A. W. Bates and J. Robinson. Milton Keynes, England: The Open University Press.

Gibb, J. R. 1961. "Defensive Behavior." *Journal of Communication* 11(3):141–48.

Gibbons, J. F.; Kincheloe, W. R.; and Down, K. S. March 18, 1977. "Tutored Videotape Instruction: A New Use of Electronics Media in Education." *Science* 5(195):1139–46.

Giltrow, D. R., and Duby, P. B. February 1978. "Predicting Student Withdrawals in Open Learning Courses." *Educational Technology* 18(2): 43–48.

Glatter, R., and Wedell, E. G. 1971. *Study by Correspondence: An Inquiry into Correspondence Study for Examinations for Degrees and Other Advanced Qualifications.* London: Longman.

Gooler, Dennis D. Summer 1979. "Evaluating Distance Education Programs." *Canadian Journal of University Continuing Education* 6(1):43–55.

Gough, J. E. August 1980a. "Listening and Learning: Audio Cassettes at Deakin University." *Open Campus* 2:7–18. Mimeographed. Geelong, Victoria, Australia: Deakin University. ED 224 430. 13 pp. MF–$1.97; PC–$3.74.

———. 1980b. "The Use of Study Centres in Four Distance Education Systems." Mimeographed. Geelong, Victoria, Australia: Deakin University. ED 220 666. 56 pp. MF–$1.17; PC–$7.24.

Gough, J. E., and Coltman, B. 1979. "Counseling the Distance Student: Fact or Fiction." *Open Campus* 2:39–47. Mimeographed. Geelong, Victoria, Australia: Deakin University. ED 227 745. 9 pp. MF–$1.17; PC–$3.74.

Graff, S. M. 1980. "Alternative Delivery Systems." In *Telecourse Reflections '80,* edited by Kiki S. Munshi. Washington, D.C.: Corporation for Public Broadcasting. ED 191 115. 142 pp. MF–$1.17; PC–$12.87.

Hamblin, Bill. 1982. "Interactive Videolaw Seminars." In *Tele-*

conferencing and Electronic Communications, edited by L. A. Parker and C. H. Olgren. Madison, Wis.: University of Wisconsin Extension.

Hammer, P., and Smith, W. A. 1979. "Attrition-Completion Study in an Open University." Paper presented at the annual forum of the Association for Institutional Research, San Diego, 13–17 May. ED 174 096. 35 pp. MF–$1.17; PC–$5.49.

Harris, W. J. 1975. "The Distance Tutor in Correspondence Education." In *The System of Distance Education.* Papers presented to the tenth ICCE International Conference, Brighton, England, 12–16 May. Malmö, Sweden: Hermods. ED 170 549. 248 pp. MF–$1.17; PC not available EDRS.

Hawkridge, D. G. 1981. "International Co-production of Distance Teaching Courses." In *Education of Adults at a Distance,* edited by Michael W. Neil. London: Kogan Page, Ltd.

Hegel, E. J. 1981. "Survey of Policies in University-Level Correspondence Programs in Canada and the United States of America." Mimeographed. Saskatoon, Saskatchewan: University of Saskatchewan.

Hewitt, Louise M., ed. 1982. *A Telecourse Sourcebook for the 80's.* Fountain Valley, Calif.: Coast Community College District.

Heydinger, Richard. 1979. "Computer Conferencing: Its Use as a Pedagogical Tool." In *Educational Futures Sourcebook I,* edited by Fred Kierstead, Jim Bowman, and Christopher Dede. Washington, D.C.: World Future Society.

Hiltz, Starr R., and Turoff, Murray. 1978. *The Network Nation.* Reading, Mass.: Addison-Wesley.

Hiscox, Michael. Spring 1982. "A Summary of the Practicality and Potential of Videodiscs in Education." *Videodisc/Videotex* 2(2):99–109.

Holmberg, Börje. June 1980. "Aspects of Distance Education." *Comparative Education* 16(2):107–19.

———. 1981. *Status and Trends of Distance Education.* New York: Nichols.

———. February 1982. *Recent Research into Distance Education.* Hagen, West Germany: Zentrales Institute für Fernstudienforschung.

Horgan, David; Nelson, Deborah; and Young, Roger. 1979. *Self-Evaluation Report: Department of Independent Study.* Minneapolis: Continuing Education and Extension Division, University of Minnesota.

Hurly, Paul; Hlynka, Denis; and Hurly, Janet. 1982. "Videotex: An Interactive Tool for Education and Training." In *Telecon-*

ferencing and Electronic Communications, edited by L. A. Parker and C. H. Olgren. Madison, Wis.: University of Wisconsin Extension.

Information Services Department. 1981. *An Introduction to the Open University.* Milton Keynes, England: The Open University.

Jackson, L. B.; Parker, L. A.; and Olgren, C. H. 1979. "Teleconferencing + Telewriting = Continuing Education in Wisconsin." In *Educational Telecommunications Delivery Systems,* edited by John A. Curtis and Joseph M. Biedenbach. Washington, D.C.: American Society for Engineering Education. ED 187 341. 152 pp. MF–$1.17; PC not available EDRS.

Jelen, Charlanne, and Hirschfield, Adele. 1978. *Handbook for Coordinated Instructional Systems Course Learning Managers.* Fountain Valley, Calif.: Coastline Community College.

Kaye, Anthony, and Rumble, Greville, eds. 1981. *Distance Teaching for Higher and Adult Education.* London: Croom Helm.

Keegan, Desmond J. 1981. *The Regional Tutorial Services of the Open University: A Case Study.* Hagen, West Germany: Fernuniversität, ZIFF.

Keegan, Desmond J., and Rumble, Greville. 1982. "The DTU's: An Appraisal." In *The Distance Teaching Universities,* edited by Greville Rumble and Keith Harry. New York: St. Martin's Press.

Kelly, J. T., and Anandam, K. 1979. "Communicating with Distant Learners." In *Using Mass Media for Learning,* edited by R. Yarrington. Washington, D.C.: American Association of Community and Junior Colleges. ED 165 856. 82 pp. MF–$1.17; PC–$9.37.

Kern, Larry. 1976. "Using Broadcasting Notes in Distance Teaching." Paper no. 69. Mimeographed. Milton Keynes, England: Institute of Educational Technology, British Open University.

Kern, Larry, and Mason, J. 1977. "Nonbroadcast Media Technologies at the OU." *Educational Broadcasting International* 10(3):106–11.

Kiesling, H. Spring 1979. "Economic Cost Analysis in Higher Education: The University of Mid-America and Traditional Institutions Compared." *Educational Communications and Technology Journal* 27(1):9–24.

King, Brenda; Sewart, David; and Gough, J. Eric. 1980. "Support Systems in Distance Education." *Open Campus* 3:13–38. Mimeographed. Geelong, Victoria, Australia: Deakin University. ED 227 746. 15 pp. MF–$1.17; PC–$3.74.

Klees, S. J. 1975. "Postsecondary Open Learning Systems: Cost-Effectiveness and Benefit Considerations." In *Designing Diver-*

sity '75, edited by C. E. Cavert. Lincoln, Neb.: University of Mid-America. ED 118 109. 411 pp. MF–$1.17; PC not available EDRS.

Knapper, Christopher, and Wills, Barry L. July/August 1980. "Educational Technology in Canada: Recent Developments and Future Trends." *Higher Education in Europe* 5(3):10–14.

Knights, S., and McDonald, R. October 1982. "Adult Learners in Higher Education: Some Study Problems and Solutions from Australian Experience." *British Journal of Educational Technology* 13(3):237–46.

Kruh, Jan. 1982. "Innovative Programming on the Kansas Regents Network (Telenet)." In *Teleconferencing and Electronic Communications,* edited by L. A. Parker and C. H. Olgren. Madison, Wis.: University of Wisconsin Extension.

Kulik, James A.; Kulik, Chen-Lin C.; and Cohen, Peter A. 1980. "Effectiveness of Computer-Based College Teaching: A Meta-analysis of Findings." *Review of Educational Research* 50(4):525–44.

Lefranc, Robert. 1982. "Cost Efficiency of University Teaching Systems at a Distance." *Educational Media International* 2:20–24.

Lehmann, Timothy. 1981. "Evaluating Adult Learning and Program Costs." In *The Modern American College,* edited by Arthur Chickering. San Francisco: Jossey-Bass.

Leverenz, Theodore. 1979. *Student Perceptions of Instructional Quality of Correspondence Study Courses.* Lexington: Independent Study Program, University of Kentucky.

Lewis, Raymond. 1983. *Meeting Learners' Needs through Telecommunications: A Directory and Guide to Programs.* Washington, D.C.: American Association for Higher Education. ED 227 746. 264 pp. MF–$1.17; PC not available EDRS.

Lewis, Roger. 1981. *How to Tutor in an Open-Learning Scheme.* London: Council of Educational Technology.

———. 1982. "The Role of the Correspondence Tutor." In *Learning at a Distance: A World Perspective,* edited by John S. Daniel, Martha A. Stroud, and John R. Thompson. Edmonton, Alberta: Athabasca University.

Lipson, Joseph. September/October 1977. "Technology and Adult Education: A Report on the University of Mid-America Experiment." *Technological Horizons in Education Journal* 4:36.

Lombardi, John. 1977. *Noncampus Colleges: New Governance Patterns for Outreach Programs.* Los Angeles: ERIC Clearinghouse for Junior Colleges. ED 136 880. 76 pp. MF–$1.17; PC–$9.37.

Lumsden, Keith, and Scott, Alex. 1982. "An Output Comparison of Open University and Conventional University Students." *Higher Education* 11:573–91.

McCabe, R. H. 1979. "The Economics of Television-Centered Courses." In *Using Mass Media for Learning,* edited by Roger Yarrington. Washington, D.C.: American Association of Community and Junior Colleges. ED 165 856. 82 pp. MF–$1.17; PC not available EDRS.

McDonald, Roland, and Knights, Sue. February 1979. "Learning from Tapes: The Experience of Home-Based Students." *Programmed Learning and Educational Technology* 16(1):46–51.

Mace, J. 1978. "Mythology in the Making: Is the Open University Really Cost-Effective?" *Higher Education* 7:295–309.

McIntosh, N. E.; Woodley, A.; and Morrison, V. 1979. "Student Demand and Progress at the Open University." Mimeographed. Paper presented at the Tenth Anniversary Conference on Education of Adults at a Distance, British Open University, Milton Keynes, England.

McIntyre, Catherine, and Wales, Christy A. 1976. *Evaluation of a Nontraditional College: Costs and Effectiveness.* Seattle: Washington Board for Community Colleges. ED 131 881. 76 pp. MF–$1.17; PC–$9.37.

MacKenzie, N.; Postgate, R.; Scupham, J. 1975. *Open Learning: Systems and Problems in Postsecondary Education.* Paris: The UNESCO Press.

Markowitz, Harold, Jr. January 1983. *Independent Study in 1982: National University Continuing Education Association Independent Study Programs.* Gainesville, Fla.: Independent Study Program, University of Florida. ED 227 801. 34 pp. MF–$1.17; PC–$5.49.

Marland, P. W., and Store, R. E. 1982. "Some Instructional Strategies for Improving Learning from Distance Teaching Materials." *Distance Education* 3(1):72–106.

Mathieson, David E. 1971. *Correspondence Study: A Summary Review of the Research and Development Literature.* Syracuse, N.Y.: Syracuse University. ED 047 163. 108 pp. MF–$1.17; PC–$11.12.

Meakin, Denys. 1982. "The Role of Regional Centres." In *Learning at a Distance: A World Perspective,* edited by John S. Daniel, Martha A. Stroud, and John R. Thompson. Edmonton, Alberta: Athabasca University.

Medsker, Leland L., and Edelstein, Stewart L. 1977. *Policy Guidelines for Extended Degree Programs: A Revision.* Washington, D.C.: American Council of Education.

Medsker, Leland L.; Edelstein, Stewart L.; Kreplin, H.; Ruyle,

J.; and Shea, J. 1975. *Extending Opportunities for a College Degree: Practices, Problems, and Potential.* Berkeley: Center for Research and Development in Higher Education. ED 125 418. 397 pp. MF–$1.17; PC–$31.90.

Meed, John R. 1977. "The Use of Radio in the Open University's Multimedia Educational System." In *Evaluating Educational Television and Radio,* edited by A. W. Bates and John Robinson. Milton Keynes, England: The Open University Press.

Miller, Philip. 1982. "Participatory Television: Education and Interactive Cable TV." In *Teleconferencing and Electronic Communications,* edited by L. A. Parker and C. H. Olgren. Madison, Wis.: University of Wisconsin Extension.

Munshi, Kiki S. 1980. *Telecourse Reflections '80.* Washington, D.C.: Corporation for Public Broadcasting. ED 191 115. 142 pp. MF–$1.17; PC–$12.87.

Nathenson, Michael B.; Brown, S.; Kirkup, G.; and Lewsey, M. May 1981. "Learning from Evaluation at the Open University I: A New Model of Course Development." *British Journal of Education Technology* 12(2):120–39.

National Public Radio Education Services. 1982. "Summary Report of the Radio/Audio Adult Learning Service Task Force." Mimeographed. Washington, D.C.: National Public Radio.

Neil, Michael W. 1981. *Education of Adults at a Distance.* London: Kogan Page Ltd.

Norwood, Frank W. 1976. "Communications Technology: Means for Outreach." In *Conference Proceedings: Forum 76,* edited by C. E. Cavert. Lincoln, Neb.: University of Mid-America.

————. 1981. "Public Telecommunications Policies and Educations Options." In *National Conference on Technology and Education,* edited by Information Dynamics, Inc. Washington, D.C.: Institute for Educational Leadership, George Washington University.

O'Rourke, James S. 1980. "Research on Telecommunications and the Adult Learner." In *Television in Community and Junior Colleges: An Overview and Guidelines,* edited by James J. Zigerell, James S. O'Rourke, and Theodore W. Pohrte. Syracuse, N.Y.: ERIC Clearinghouse on Information Resources, Syracuse University. ED 206 329. 46 pp. MF–$1.17; PC–$5.49.

Orton, L. J. Summer 1977. "Completion and Nonstart Rates in Correspondence Courses." *Canadian Journal of University Continuing Education* 4(1):21–26.

Peruniak, Geoff. 1980. "Seminars as an Instructional Strategy in Distance Education." Mimeographed. Edmonton, Alberta: Athabasca University.

Reed, Bill. 18 June 1982. "PBS Adult Learning Service: First Year Report." Mimeographed. Washington, D.C.: Public Broadcasting Service.

Rekkedal, Torstein. 1982. "The Dropout Problem and What to Do about It." In *Learning at a Distance: A World Perspective,* edited by John S. Daniel, Martha A. Stroud, and John R. Thompson. Edmonton, Alberta: Athabasca University.

Ruggles, R. H. 1982. *Learning at a Distance and the New Technology.* Vancouver, B.C.: Educational Research Institute of British Columbia.

Sakamoto, Takashi. 1982. "Plan to Reality: The Japan University of the Air." In *Learning at a Distance: A World Perspective,* edited by John S. Daniel, Martha A. Stroud, and John R. Thompson. Edmonton, Alberta: Athabasca University.

Salter, Don. 1982. "Mobile Learning Centres in an Open Learning System." In *Learning at a Distance: A World Perspective,* edited by John S. Daniel, Martha A. Stroud, and John R. Thompson. Edmonton, Alberta: Athabasca University.

Salvaggio, Jerry L. 1982. "An Assessment of Japan As an Information Society in the 1980's." In *Communications and the Future: Prospects, Promises, and Problems,* edited by H. F. Didsbury. Bethesda, Md.: World Future Society.

Schaie, K. Warner, and Parr, Joyce. 1981. "Intelligence." In *The Modern American College,* edited by Arthur Chickering and Associates. San Francisco: Jossey-Bass.

Schramm, Wilbur. 1977. *Big Media, Little Media.* Beverly Hills, Calif.: Sage Publications.

Sewart, David. 1975. "Some Observations on the Formation of Study Groups." *Teaching at a Distance* 2.

Shale, D. G. 1982. "Attrition: A Case Study." In *Learning at a Distance: A World Perspective,* edited by John S. Daniel, Martha A. Stroud, and John R. Thompson. Edmonton, Alberta: Athabasca University.

Sharples, Mike. 1982. "An Evaluation of the CYCLOPS Telewriting System for Distance Tutoring of Open University Students." In *Teleconferencing and Electronic Communications,* edited by L. A. Parker and C. H. Olgren. Madison, Wis.: University of Wisconsin Extension.

Short, S.H. 1977. "A Comparison of Variable Time-Compressed Speech and Normal Rate Speech Based on the Time Spent and Performance in a Course Taught by Self-Instructional Methods." *British Journal of Educational Technology* 8(2): 146–57.

Smith, Gregory. December 1980. "Informing and Advising Americans at Work: Hard Evidence That It Matters and Works."

National Center for Educational Brokering Bulletin 5(10):1–4.

Smith, Kevin C., and Small, Ian W. 1982. "Student Support: How Much Is Enough?" In *Learning at a Distance: A World Perspective,* edited by John A. Daniel, Martha A. Stroud, and John R. Thompson. Edmonton, Alberta: Athabasca University.

Sosdian, Carol P. March 1978. *External Degrees: Program and Student Characteristics.* Washington, D.C.: National Institute of Education. ED 152 174. 65 pp. MF–$1.17; PC–$7.62.

Stanford, J. D., and Imrie, B. W. October 1981. "A Three-stage Evaluation of a Distance Education Course." *British Journal of Educational Technology* 12(3):198–210.

Stoane, C., and Stoane, J. S. 1982. "Answers at a Distance." In *Aspects of Educational Technology,* edited by F. Percival and H. Ellington. London: Kogan Page.

Store, R. E., and Armstrong, J. D. May 1981. "Personalizing Feedback between Teacher and Student in the Context of a Particular Model of Distance Teaching." *British Journal of Educational Technology* 12(2):140–57.

Szilak, Dennis. April 1979. "Interactive Tape Cassettes for Industrial Training." *Educational and Industrial Television* 11(4): 43–44.

Thorton, Robert, and Mitchell, Ian. 1978. *Counseling the Distance Learner: A Survey of Trends and Literature.* Adelaide, South Australia: Adelaide University. ED 177 296. 37 pp. MF–$1.17; PC–$5.49.

Wagner, Leslie. 1977. "The Economics of the Open University Revisited." *Higher Education* 6:359–81.

Walker, Mike. 1982. "Local Support for the Local Learner." In *Learning at a Distance: A World Perspective,* edited by John S. Daniel, Martha A. Stroud, and John R. Thompson. Edmonton, Alberta: Athabasca University.

Waniewicz, Ignacy. 1979. "Developing Adult Distance Learning As a Collaborative Venture." Mimeographed. Paper presented at the Tenth Anniversary Conference of the British Open University. Milton Keynes, England: British Open University.

———. June 1981. "The TV Ontario Academy: The Use of Television Broadcasting and Computer-managed Learning for Adults." *Educational Broadcasting International* 14(2):78–81.

Weber, Larry J.; McBee, Janice K.; and Krebs, Jean E. 1982. "Take-home Tests: An Experimental Study." Mimeographed. Paper presented at the annual meeting of the American Educational Research Association, New York, March.

Weingartz, Monika. 1981. "ZIFF Research on Distance Education." *Distance Education* 2(2):240–48.

Wertheim, Judith B. 1981. "The Medium Is . . . Nontraditional

---

Approach to Counseling Adult Learners." In *Advising and Counseling Adult Learners*, edited by Frank DiSilvestro. San Francisco: Jossey-Bass.

Woolfe, Roger. November 1981. "Videotex and Teletext: Similarities, Differences, and Prospects." *Programmed Learning and Educational Technology* 18(4):245–52.

Zigerell, James. February 1982. "Consortia: A Grow Trend in Educational Programming." *Educational/Industrial Television* 14(2):43–47.

ASHE-ERIC Higher Education Research Reports

Starting in 1983 the Association for the Study of Higher Education assumed cosponsorship of the Higher Education Research Reports with the ERIC Clearinghouse on Higher Education. For the previous 11 years ERIC and the American Association for Higher Education prepared and published the reports.

Each report is the definitive analysis of a tough higher education problem, based on a thorough research of pertinent literature and institutional experiences. Report topics, identified by a national survey, are written by noted practitioners and scholars with prepublication manuscript reviews by experts.

Ten monographs in the ASHE-ERIC Higher Education Research Report series are published each year, available individually or by subscription. Subscription to 10 issues is $50 regular; $35 for members of AERA, AAHE, and AIR; $30 for members of ASHE. (Add $7.50 outside U.S.)

Prices for single copies, including 4th class postage and handling, are $6.50 regular and $5.00 for members of AERA, AAHE, AIR, and ASHE. If faster first-class postage is desired for U.S. and Canadian orders, add $.60 per report; for overseas, add $4.50. For VISA and Master-Card payments, give card number, expiration date, and signature. Orders under $25 must be prepaid. Bulk discounts are available on orders of 25 or more of a single title. Order from the Publications Department, Association for the Study of Higher Education, One Dupont Circle, Suite 630, Washington, D.C. 20036, (202) 296-2597. Write for a complete list of Higher Education Research Reports and other ASHE and ERIC publications.

1981 Higher Education Research Reports

1. Minority Access to Higher Education
   Jean L. Preer

2. Institutional Advancement Strategies in Hard Times
   Michael D. Richards and Gerald Sherratt

3. Functional Literacy in the College Setting
   Richard C. Richardson, Jr., Kathryn J. Martens, and Elizabeth C. Fisk

4. Indices of Quality in the Undergraduate Experience
   George D. Kuh

5. Marketing in Higher Education
   Stanley M. Grabowski

6. Computer Literacy in Higher Education
   Francis E. Masat

---

7. Financial Analysis for Academic Units
   Donald L. Walters

8. Assessing the Impact of Faculty Collective Bargaining
   J. Victor Baldridge, Frank K. Kemerer, and Associates

9. Strategic Planning, Management, and Decision Making
   Robert G. Cope

10. Organizational Communication in Higher Education
    Robert D. Gratz and Philip J. Salem

1982 Higher Education Research Reports

1. Rating College Teaching: Criterion Studies of Student Evaluation-of-Instruction Instruments
   Sidney E. Benton

2. Faculty Evaluation: The Use of Explicit Criteria for Promotion, Retention, and Tenure
   Neal Whitman and Elaine Weiss

3. The Enrollment Crisis: Factors, Actors, and Impacts
   J. Victor Baldridge, Frank R. Kemerer, and Kenneth C. Green

4. Improving Instruction: Issues and Alternatives for Higher Education
   Charles C. Cole, Jr.

5. Planning for Program Discontinuance: From Default to Design
   Gerlinda S. Melchiori

6. State Planning, Budgeting, and Accountability: Approaches for Higher Education
   Carol E. Floyd

7. The Process of Change in Higher Education Institutions
   Robert C. Nordvall

8. Information Systems and Technological Decisions: A Guide for Non-Technical Administrators
   Robert L. Bailey

9. Government Support for Minority Participation in Higher Education
   Kenneth C. Green

10. The Department Chair: Professional Development and Role Conflict
    David B. Booth

1983 Higher Education Research Reports

1. The Path to Excellence: Quality Assurance in Higher Education
   Laurence R. Marcus, Anita O. Leone, and Edward D. Goldberg

2. Faculty Recruitment, Retention, and Fair Employment: Obligations and Opportunities
   John S. Waggaman

3. Meeting the Challenges: Developing Faculty Careers
   Michael C. T. Brookes and Katherine L. German

4. Raising Academic Standards: A Guide to Learning Improvement
   Ruth Talbott Keimig

5. Serving Learners at a Distance: A Guide to Program Practices
   Charles E. Feasley